D1565009

BRONSON

From the Belly of the Beast to Freedom

BRONSON FRANK

Copyright 2020, Bronson Frank.

All rights reserved. No parts of this book may be reproduced or transmitted in
any form or by any means without the expressed written permission of the author.
Requests for permission should be addressed to bronsonf7@gmail.com.

BRONSON: From the Belly of the Beast to Freedom
ISBN: 9798702102399

Cover and interior design by Stephanie Whitlock Dicken.
Edited by Bethany Bradsher.

All rights reserved worldwide.

The Belly of the Beast

FRANK! 88T1199! BANG!! That was the loud sound of the gate that closed behind me after I heard a correctional officer yell my inmate number when I was locked up in my first facility. I was convicted of a sex offense and given an eight-and-a-half to twenty-five-year sentence. My case involved two college females at the local college. B block, second floor, Tier 4, 7 cell, Southport Correctional Facility became my new home in October 1988. I will never forget the sound of that gate closing behind me.

I adjusted quickly to a life that was to be mine for the next twenty years. My first thought was, "I am locked in and I cannot get out." Obviously, my life changed completely. On my first walk down the tier I noticed how the other inmates had their cells set up; they looked like mini-apartments. Well I guess that is really what they were—home. A temporary home away from home. I was immediately accepted because I was a good basketball player. I hung with the basketball players and they taught me the ropes. The prison was approximately sixty percent black, thirty-five percent Hispanic and five percent white. The noise level was deafening.

One of the basketball player inmates I met was named Mo. Joe Mobley was his actual name. Sometimes he was friendly and sometimes, he intimidated me. We became close friends. After being there a few months I was approached by a much more experienced guy, a Hispanic inmate named Nick Robles, asking me to be a part of the Prison Inmate Liaison Committee. I accepted, and I was given a pass to go around the facility to help with prison issues. Having a pass to go throughout the facility was a privilege. I was privileged to be accepted by guys who had been in prison for ten to fifteen years, who were a part of the liaison committee. A lot of guys were jealous and wanted that privilege, to have access throughout the whole facility. I was allowed to go to all three blocks — A, B and C blocks.

My first awakening came when my cell was robbed at the Southport C.F. It was probably my sixth month of being incarcerated. I knew who took my things but there wasn't much I could do. I had no backup and knew no one who would help me. So I was told to leave it alone and take it as a learning experience. Ramen noodles were called crackhead soup. I have had my share, but I haven't eaten it once since I got home. I honestly would not mind one today. Along with a peanut butter and jelly sandwich. It was good. I can't forget all of the tuna sandwiches also. A honeybun was usually the desert.

Southport Correctional held approximately 1,500 inmates. It was just outside of Elmira, N.Y. in a small town called Pine City. It was a brand-new facility, and I arrived there in October 1988. In June 1990 there was a racial riot at Southport. Seeing 100 Hispanic and 100 black inmates running towards each other to fight, stab, and cut was a very scary sight. I remember the officers shooting their guns from the towers and dumping tear gas on the rioters. I remember jumping on top of a table with five other guys to get out of the way of the fighting and stabbing. I can still hear the sounds of guys getting stabbed. Everyone had to get on the ground for approximately two hours before everyone was finally led back to their cell.

The riot continued for at least forty-five minutes. I had heard there were racial problems between the black and Hispanic inmates, and a Spanish kid named Carlos told me that day that there were going to be problems between the two groups. He suggested that I go at the other end of the yard to be away from it. I did. I thought racial stuff was between the blacks and the whites, not the blacks and Hispanics. The facility was in lockdown for about two weeks after that but having the liaison pass allowed me to still go throughout the facility. There were only four other guys who had passes who were allowed out of our cells and go to the other blocks. We had to eat bagged lunches for two weeks, and guys were placed in the box — S.H.U. Special Housing Unit, also known as isolation — because they were involved in the riot, some for years. Some of the correctional officers (COs) were also injured during the riot.

As time went on, I realized that even though the Hispanics were outnumbered by the blacks they won most of the fights, because they stuck together more than us blacks did. The blacks did not begin getting respect until 1996 and 1997, when the Bloods started coming into play. I was thankful in a sense, because I was tired of seeing the blacks being disrespected so much. It was the blacks' turn to get some respect and get some payback. Southport Correctional Facility was a learning experience for me, as it prepared me for the many facilities and situations to come. I learned about gangs, which they call families. I learned about weapons such as a razor (ox) and a banger (ice pick). It taught me how to detect a real friend from a phony friend. I was well-seasoned when I was transferred out of Southport in early 1991.

Through my twenty-plus years behind bars, I spent time in eighteen different prison facilities. My incarceration began in 1988 at O.C.J., the Ontario County Jail. Being sentenced to eight-and-a-half to twenty-five years, I never imagined I would end up completing more than twenty years. I pleaded guilty to two counts of sodomy – two four-and-a-half to twelve-and-a-half-year sentences, which equaled the total years of my sentence. The type of sodomy was oral sex. While at the county jail I was told by my attorney that he could get my sentenced reduced to four years for another $1,000. We got him the money, but we never heard much from him after that.

BRONSON FRANK SENTENCING

Statewide Criminal History in New York for BRONSON T FRANK -hits :

Search Type : Felony Including Misdemeanor

Case #88-04-134

Case Number	88-04-134
Source	COUNTY COURT
Jurisdiction	ONTARIO
Source State	NY
Offense Date	05/26/1988
Disposition Date	10/26/1988

Defendant :BRONSON THOMAS FRANK
DOB   02/20/1956
Identified by : name, date of birth

Charge #1	
Charge	1ST DEGREE - SODOMY
Crime Type	FELONY - CLASS B
Disposition	PLED GUILTY
Statute	PL 130.50 01
Plea	GUILTY

Sentence Comments : SENTENCED TO: IMPRISONMENT 4 YEARS 3 MONTHS - 12 YEARS 9 MONTHS

Charge #2	
Charge	1ST DEGREE - SODOMY
Crime Type	FELONY - CLASS B
Disposition	PLED GUILTY
Statute	PL 130.50 01
Plea	GUILTY

Sentence Comments : SENTENCED TO: IMPRISONMENT 4 YEARS 3 MONTHS - 12 YEARS 9 MONTHS

BRONSON

Charge #3

Charge	1ST DEGREE - SODOMY
Crime Type	FELONY - CLASS B
Disposition	PLED GUILTY
Statute	PL 130.50 01
Plea	GUILTY

Sentence Comments : SENTENCED TO: IMPRISONMENT 4 YEARS 3 MONTHS - 12 YEARS 9 MONTHS

Charge #4

Charge	2ND DEGREE - BURGLARY
Crime Type	FELONY - CLASS C
Disposition	PLED GUILTY
Statute	PL 140.25 02
Plea	GUILTY

Sentence Comments : SENTENCED TO: IMPRISONMENT 3 YEARS - 9 YEARS, FINAL ORDER OF PROTECTION, 12 YEARS

Charge #5

Charge	2ND DEGREE - BURGLARY
Crime Type	FELONY - CLASS C
Disposition	PLED GUILTY
Statute	PL 140.25 02
Plea	GUILTY

Sentence Comments : SENTENCED TO: IMPRISONMENT 3 YEARS - 9 YEARS, FINAL ORDER OF PROTECTION, 12 YEARS

Charge #6

Charge	2ND DEGREE - BURGLARY
Crime Type	FELONY - CLASS C
Disposition	PLED GUILTY
Statute	PL 140.25 02
Plea	GUILTY

Sentence Comments : SENTENCED TO: IMPRISONMENT 3 YEARS - 9 YEARS, FINAL ORDER OF PROTECTION, 12 YEARS

Charge #7

Charge	3RD DEGREE - ASSAULT
Crime Type	MISDEMEANOR - CLASS A
Disposition	PLED GUILTY
Statute	PL 120.00 01
Plea	GUILTY

Sentence Comments : SENTENCED TO: UNCONDITIONAL DISCHARGE

Charge #8

Charge	PETIT LARCENY
Crime Type	MISDEMEANOR - CLASS A
Disposition	PLED GUILTY
Statute	PL 155.25 00
Plea	GUILTY

Sentence Comments : SENTENCED TO: UNCONDITIONAL DISCHARGE

Charge #9

Charge	1ST DEGREE - BURGLARY
Crime Type	FELONY - CLASS B
Disposition	PLED GUILTY
Statute	PL 140.30 02
Plea	GUILTY

Sentence Comments : SENTENCED TO: IMPRISONMENT 3 YEARS 4 MONTHS - 10 YEARS

6

Charge #10

Charge	1ST DEGREE - SEXUAL ABUSE
Crime Type	FELONY - CLASS D
Disposition	PLED GUILTY
Statute	PL 130.65 01
Plea	GUILTY

Sentence Comments : SENTENCED TO: IMPRISONMENT 1 YEAR 4 MONTHS - 4 YEARS

Charge #11

Charge	1ST DEGREE - ATTEMPTED SEXUAL ABUSE
Crime Type	FELONY - CLASS E
Disposition	PLED GUILTY
Statute	PL 110-130.65 01
Plea	GUILTY

Sentence Comments : SENTENCED TO: IMPRISONMENT 1 YEAR - 3 YEARS

Charge #12

Charge	2ND DEGREE - ASSAULT
Crime Type	FELONY - CLASS D
Disposition	PLED GUILTY
Statute	PL 120.05 06
Plea	GUILTY

Sentence Comments : SENTENCED TO: IMPRISONMENT 1 YEAR 4 MONTHS - 4 YEARS

Charge #13

Charge	1ST DEGREE - ATTEMPTED RAPE
Crime Type	FELONY - CLASS C
Disposition	PLED GUILTY
Statute	PL 110-130.35 01
Plea	GUILTY

Sentence Comments : SENTENCED TO: IMPRISONMENT 3 YEAR - 9 YEARS

I waited in the Ontario County Jail for approximately three weeks before being transferred to Downstate Correctional Facility, a transfer facility where most inmates go for preparation to prison. Downstate was located in Malone, N.Y. in Franklin County, south of Poughkeepsie. I was only there for a few days before I was transferred to my first Prison — Southport Correctional Facility. I went there with another guy from Geneva – Jesse Smallwood. Guys who are seasoned knew if you are new to the system or not. They knew I was new, I realized they were reading me by the way I was talking.

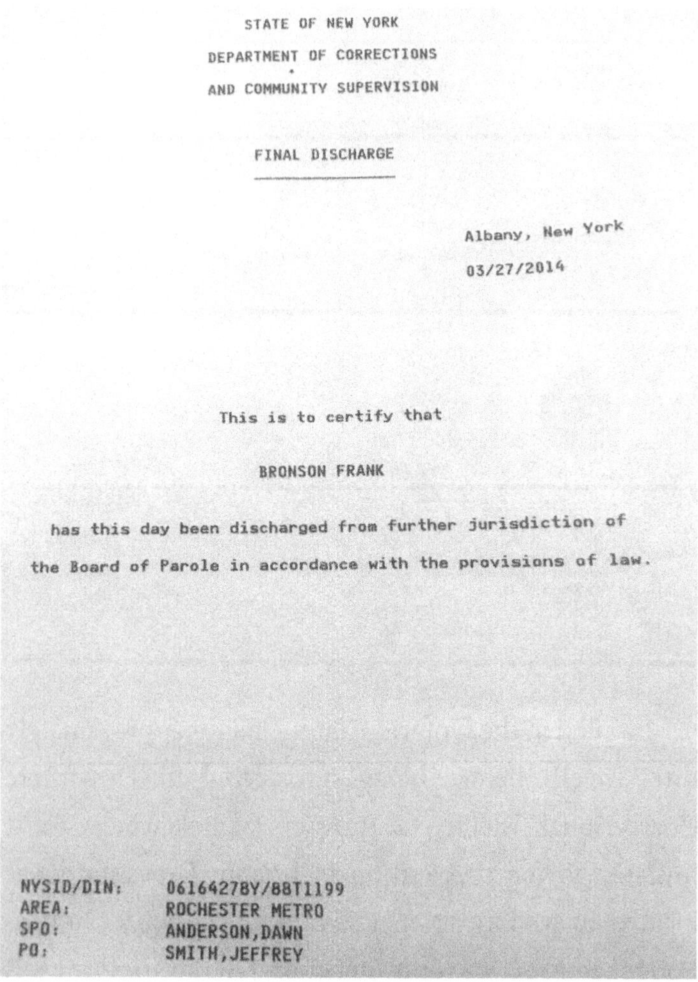

STATE OF NEW YORK

DEPARTMENT OF CORRECTIONS

AND COMMUNITY SUPERVISION

FINAL DISCHARGE

Albany, New York

03/27/2014

This is to certify that

BRONSON FRANK

has this day been discharged from further jurisdiction of
the Board of Parole in accordance with the provisions of law.

NYSID/DIN:	06164278Y/88T1199
AREA:	ROCHESTER METRO
SPO:	ANDERSON,DAWN
PO:	SMITH,JEFFREY

I talked different, I had an upstate accent, or I spoke like
I was white. Walking into the cafeteria the next morning
I first noticed how many faces were black compared to
white. I think I saw maybe four white faces in all the
black and Hispanic faces.

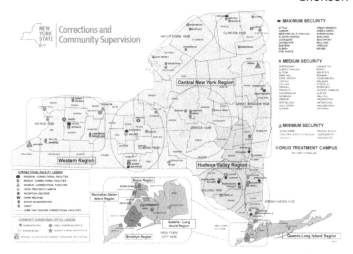

In my role on the liaison committee, I mostly transported cigarettes or marijuana from dorm to dorm and passed cigarettes from cell to cell. I did what I could do for both families — black and Hispanic. Before leaving Southport C.F. on February 20, 1991 my then-girlfriend Lisa Alexander decided to stop coming to see me. She told me she found another guy and she was not coming back. She was not nasty about it and I respected her for it. I thought I would be OK, but when she left my world went into a tailspin. I was in a tailspin for approximately six months, but I finally came out of it.

Again, my girlfriend Lisa Alexander had been coming to visit me most every weekend. I would always encourage her to go her way and leave me. There was not much I could do for her, since I was facing many more years in prison. I would tell her that this was my fight and she did not deserve to be a part of it. "Go and find a nice guy who can treat you better than me," is what I told her. On my birthday, February 20, 1991, she left me. My world was in a spin for about six months. She soon married the neighbor. Lisa was my biggest loss. I finally came out of that spin and started my journey in the Prison system – (aka) The Belly of the Beast.

Lisa was the best and I 'fucked up' a good thing with her. If I knew then what I know now I would have married her the first day we met. An awesome lady, Lisa was also a Geneva girl—a 1984 GHS graduate and an extremely beautiful Italian lady. One thing I will always respect Lisa for was when her dad told her he would wash his hands of her if she continued to date me – a black man. She stuck to her guns and continued to date me. She did not hear much from her mom for approximately six months after we started dating, and her mom finally called and spoke with her. I admired her so much for that. Her favorite song is by Whitney Houston—"The Greatest Love of All." That song spoke about following your own dreams and not living your life for others. Even though her parents wanted her to stop seeing me, she decided to never walk in anyone's shadow, and never walk in another's dream. She wanted to walk in her own dream, not follow the dreams of others.

7-1-89

Lisa and Me

Lisa and Me

Lisa learned to love herself – it was her greatest love of all. I was not ready for Lisa. She thought deeply. I was not at her level. I will always compare our relationship like that of NBA Player Tony Parker and Model Eva Longoria. Lisa was fashion, fame – lights, camera, action. I was like Tony Parker, a playboy who still wanted to play around. Lisa was NBA status and I was ABA status. That's why it didn't work. Lisa had three sisters and one brother. Her sister's Carol and Linda were supportive and Diane was not. Her brother Bob seemed supportive also. Lisa was not only physically beautiful – she was more beautiful inside. She was a very caring and loving person. I lost an angel. As she would say, I lost a gem. A true statement.

BRONSON

Life on the Inside

In 1991 I left Southport Correctional Facility and was shipped to my next prison, Wende Correctional Facility in Alden, New York, in Erie County near Buffalo. Wende was one of the better facilities. They had televisions in the cells; they cost $60, and you could usually pick one up from a guy who was transferring or leaving the facility. I got a TV for two packs of Newport cigarettes. Wende C.F. had a lot of black COs (correctional officers), and that helped. Again, I started playing ball and working out with the weights pretty hard. I again was chosen for the all-star basketball team (also known as the outside team). There were also a lot of black female COs, and when they walked down the tiers you could see guys holding their mirrors out after they walked by, looking at their asses. Some of the black female officers were having sex with guys for money and commissary. I saw guys having sex with female prison guards and guys buying food items in the commissary only to give to the guards to take home. (Money talked). While at Wende I ran into Richard Fowler, who I grew up with in Geneva. Richard was the most notorious tough guy, gangster, and nice guy in Geneva history. Years later, he died in prison refereeing a basketball game. He was a Geneva legend. I joined my first Sex Offender Program at Wende. I was there for approximately one year, and I was glad to leave because it was boring.

After Wende C.F., in 1991 I went to Auburn Correctional Facility Located in Auburn New York, it was another maximum-security facility. I loved Auburn Correctional; it was much larger than the other facilities, with over 2,500 inmates. It had the best ballplayers and competition I would ever face, and some of the most notorious killers, thugs, kingpins and lifers in New York State. We had games outside in the yard in front of at least 1,000 guys watching the games. It felt like playing in a small park with 1,000 spectators — playing between four housing complexes six floors high. They would also have a baseball game going on at the same time. Some baseball shots went over the thirty-foot-high wall. Loved it. Exciting. Electric.

The yard was approximately three acres. Playing ball in the middle of the prison outside on a nice hot summer day with over 1,000 prisoners watching and yelling was one of the highlights of my career. Playing in front of 1,000 inmates outside in the yard in a prison setting is what you call 'pressure'. Being at the foul line and having a hundred inmates yelling, "Frank is a bum! Frank is gonna sell out, bet two packs he misses!" and on and on. That is what you call pressure. When I first got to Auburn C.F. I remember walking into the gym as an inmate and realizing I had been in that very gym before as a civilian. I used to schedule games for us guys from Geneva to come in and play games against the prisoners around 1977–'78. Now here I was, walking in there as a prisoner.

My cell was in block A, floor 6, ward 5, cell 27. The sixth floor was good. We could see over the wall into the streets – Routes 5 and 20. I, along with the others, would stare into freedom every day. It helped to get out of the prison mentally. It was also good because we could smoke our weed in peace; most officers did not care. I had a job in the plate shop that made the New York state license plates. Auburn was where I saw my first transgender guy/girl. I could not believe a man could look so close to looking like a female. He was Latino, and his name was Cee Cee. I have to say he/she was beautiful. Cee Cee approached me one day wanting to look at some magazines I had, since my family used to bring me magazines like "Vogue."

Kenny Gilmore was a high-ranking inmate there. He liked me because I was a good basketball player. He did not have the look of being dangerous, but he was. RobO was a dark-skinned black guy who I played basketball against. He dated a transgender boy/girl who was nice and friends with everybody. P-Funk was another ball player from Brooklyn. He was heavyset, and he used to thank me for helping him to lose weight because we usually guarded each other. We were also in the same block with inmates who were transferring. I used to keep milk in the cartons, and when they turned sour P-Funk would have me drop a sour milk in front of their cell; it was a horrible smell. Herman Henson was a well-respected guy who also played ball. He was physical like I was, and we'd get physical in the paint. Herman was a jail-house legend and did over 20 years; he was a good guy. Joe Lewis was also a prison legend, he was well known in New York City and he played basketball against Julius Erving and Kareem Abdul-Jabbar. He played in the Ruckus basketball tournament in NYC, and he used to tell me many stories about his playing days in the city. I was honored when he was the first person to ask me to play on his team.

Auburn was where I say my first guy get cut with a razor. We had an 'Upstate' basketball team, and some guys from New York City were saying that upstate guys were not as good as the NYC downstate players. They later swallowed those words. We got an all-upstate team of guys from Buffalo, Rochester, Albany and Syracuse. We were winning a lot of games and tournaments, and the other prisoners there wanted us to dismantle the upstate team. We did not dismantle. During my years of playing basketball I was nicknamed 'Frank The Tank' because of my physical playing style. Being a Veteran player, I noticed guys from NYC played with more finesse and their ball handling skills were unbelievable. Us guys from upstate N.Y. played more physical and were better jump shooters. I even noticed a difference between Rochester and Syracuse players. When I left a year later, I heard they still had the upstate team we started. I was shipped out of Auburn and hated leaving there. Being in Auburn is when I noticed many 'lifers,' the guys who were in prison for life. I also noticed guys who had been in prison for many years—fifteen, twenty, twenty-five and more years. At times you could tell by looking at them or hearing them speak. Doing time in prison is mentally challenging once you get past ten years. I knew guys who mentally were not able to do time. One day they would start talking and making no sense — that was the pressure of doing time. I have always said that I am blessed to have done 20-plus years and still have my senses – I think.

My mom passed while I was in Auburn C.F., on December 14, 1991. It was hard, but I got through it. The top Hispanic leader at the Auburn C.F. was an inmate named Al Lopez (Ally Al). He was in charge of the Latin Kings and Rat Hunters, and he liked me because I played ball well. We were also in Southport and Wende together. He came to my cell after my sister Barbara and her husband David had given me the bad news. To help me get through it. I will speak more about her passing and more about Al later in this book. I remember a Hispanic guy named Cali. He was Colombian and he was notorious. He was known for going around and robbing guys' cells. It was rumored he was a hit man for the Colombian cartel. He, along with some Puerto Rican thugs, used to extort the Dominican inmates. At that time the Dominicans were not very strong, but years later the "Dominican power" group came into effect.

The Dominicans would get extorted because they did not fight back, and most of them were in prison because they sold a lot of cocaine, so they had the money. They were targets for the Hispanic thugs. Years later I heard that the Dominicans finally got tired of Cali extorting them and six Dominicans got knives and ice picks, stabbed Cali up really bad and paralyzed him. Cali later died from his injuries. Auburn Correctional Facility was also the first place I saw guys having sex with their wives and girlfriends in the visiting room. Some were actually on the floor under their tables. Some guys did not like to, because there were kids or guys' parents there. Some guys did not care. They hadn't had sex in many years, so if the opportunity came they took it, no matter who was watching. I saw guys behind the soda machines having sex with their wives or girlfriends. Some officers understood and kept a blind eye to it.

I also got into my first fight at Auburn. Some coward, a white guy who used the Muslim faith for protection, asked me if I was gay. I immediately punched him. He swung back but missed. I punched him a few more times, and the officers were there. They put us both against the wall and took us back to our cells. I received two weeks loss of recreation and a one month loss of commissary. A lot of guys, white and black, came to prison and became Muslim for protection. I saw that White Muslim guy years later in Mid-State correctional, and he was not a Muslim anymore. I would harass him about using the Muslim faith for protection and repeatedly called him a coward for taking off his cufi once he was in a safer, medium-security prison.

In 1994, after Auburn Correctional Facility, I was sent to my first medium prison, Cayuga Correctional Facility. By then I was a seasoned veteran. The correctional officers at Cayuga, which was near Auburn C.F., had some

19

of the worst COs that I had to deal with. It was a small facility, about 700 guys. Cayuga was located 30 minutes from Auburn Correctional. Medium facilities have a much more relaxed atmosphere. Us maximum-facility guys noticed how the kids would occasionally walk by and accidentally bump into us – without saying excuse me or pardon me. That was a major mistake. The dorm situation was different also. We were housed in a dorm with another sixty or seventy guys, double-bunked. It was noisy, and we did not like it. We much preferred our own cell, for privacy. However, the food was a lot better at Cayuga. Being incarcerated, you needed outside help from friends or family to assist you with money, food and clothing. I was very lucky to have that in my early years.

Cayuga was where I had my second fight. Some Muslim guy, who I used to abuse on the basketball court, told me I had sugar in my tank. I ignored him, but the second time I punched his ass with a straight right hand. We both went to the box – isolation. I was in the box for about three weeks and then let out into population. Usually when you have a problem with Muslims, you have big problems. But because I was well-liked and the Muslim guy I punched in the face was not well-liked in the Muslim community or in population, some of the Muslims thanked me for beating his ass. The COs at Cayuga were jerks. I had problems with a few. They were punks in uniforms. Once a CO. called me a rapist, nigger, and tree jumper in front of a lot of other inmates. A 'tree jumper' is a person who jumps out of a tree onto a girl and rapes her. I reported this to a lieutenant, and I asked him to ship me out. Two days later, I was being shipped out to Mid-State Correctional Facility.

In 1995 I went to Mid-State Correctional Facility, another medium prison located in Marcy, New York just outside of Utica. It was a bad place for inmates, because the correctional officers were not nice. You did not want to get into any problems with the COs there. It was cool and quiet. I had joined my second sex offender program. I had my third fight in Mid-State. I punched some smart mouth punk over the TV and went to the box. I was there for about two months. I went to the box during summer months. Summer, depending on the facility, was the worst time to go to the box. Guy's would go to the box on purpose during the fall and winter months, just to get away from it all. When it was eighty degrees outside it was even hotter in the S.H.U. (special housing unit), or isolation cells. They made us keep our entire uniform on. Bastards…It was so damn hot in those cells. Guys were getting killed in the box. Five or six officers would choke them out and they would die. They were cowards. Before beating your ass, they would handcuff you first.

I got into the computer drafting program at Mid-State and enjoyed it. I was there until 1996. I was shipped out of Mid-State but had to finish my S.H.U., so I had box time at my next facility — Orleans Correctional Facility. I had to finish the time I was given for the fight. Orleans had the notorious Box 2000 for isolation. The women's facility, Albion Correctional, was across the fence, and we had a clear view from the second floor of S.H.U. When the sun hit their cells around 6:30 you had a clear view of the female inmates. They knew it and would wave their bras and panties. They would also wave their bras and panties out of their windows. We were told the female prisons are worse than the guys' prison. They were right. It seemed like every day we saw a female inmate being escorted to their box. Guys were talking to the girls across the fence and exchanging addresses, that's how close we were. During my five months in their box I was housed with two guys. One was a Spanish gang member. He was cool.

After he left, I got some rowdy young kid. He used to, as we would say, "stay on the gate." That meant he was always talking to some of his friends down the hall through the gate. At times it got loud in that little metal-walled six-by-nine cell. The noise would bounce off the walls, and it hurt my ears. I told him that it was bothering me and asked him to try not to yell and talk so damn long on the gate. I wanted to rest and read. I told him that he could talk to his friends for a couple of hours per day and that was it. That lasted for about a week, and then he got brave and wanted to test me. He wanted to stand in front of the mirror and rap. I asked him to stop after an hour or so. I gave him his time, since we shared that cell. After an hour I said "OK, I want to rest and read; you've had your hour." He took his shirt off, which was a sign that he was ready to fight. That is the number one rule – take your shirt off if you are going to fight. That prevents your opponent from holding you. I asked him twice to stop, and he would not. He had headphones on and was still singing and rapping in front of the mirror. I stood up from the bed and slapped him in the side of the head. I broke his headphones and knocked two braids out of his hair.

He tried to fight me back, but I was too big for him. He was a young kid, and he tried. Not only was I bigger than him, I knew how to use my size against someone smaller than me while inside of six-by-nine cell. It's a different fight in a cage that size. You had to remember where the toilet was, because it's a tripping hazard. You can also use it to your advantage. I guess my basketball skills helped me control him physically. I grabbed him with both hands on his throat. I overpowered him, punched him a few more times and he gave up. I told him to get his ass up in his bunk and shut the fuck up. I did not want to hear another word from him. He did as he was told. He got up into his bunk and went to sleep. I completed five months out of six and was shipped to the worst prison in upstate New York area – Gowanda.

Fights and Frustrations

In 1995 I was shipped to Gowanda Correctional Facility, which is located in Erie County. Again, when I left Orleans I passed through Geneva down Highway 5 and Highway 20. First I had to go to Auburn Correctional Facility, which was the transfer facility. Passing through Geneva was embarrassing. Being shackled to another guy's ankles with approximately 100 other guys was not fun. The bus would come from Auburn through Seneca Falls and Waterloo to Geneva. I grew up on Middle and Evans street, and we actually passed by the house I grew up in while I was shackled. The bus turned by the Denny's restaurant and then headed towards Penn Yan. In Gowanda, inmates were getting their asses beaten on a regular basis by the officers, and most of those officers were white and racist. Gowanda Correctional was by far the worse facility where I served time.

It was so bad that I came up with a plan. I went to Mental Health and lied, telling them I needed medication. They had a rule at Gowanda – they did not give out mental health medication. I complained to my counselor that I needed medication for my mental health issue, and she said she knew that I was lying but she still had to ship me out after that request. I was then shipped to Marcy Correctional Facility in Oneida County for a short time. It was one of the better facilities, small and quiet. After leaving Marcy I got lucky and landed in Groveland Correctional Facility.

In 1996 I was shipped to Groveland Correctional Facility, located in Sonyea, New York, near Rochester. Once again, I remember riding the bus, shackled with another 80 guys, and passing down Routes 5 and 20. From that road I could see most of Geneva. The bus always made that turn just after Denny's, on Route 14A, headed towards Penn Yan. I would see the house I grew up in on Middle and Evans Streets, and I felt shame. It seemed like every time I transferred from one facility to another I passed through my hometown, which made my situation that much more difficult to face. Groveland was definitely the best medium facility in upstate New York. It really did not have a fence. It reminded me of a college campus. It had approximately 1,500 inmates. There were about five other guys from Geneva that were there: Larry Mallard, Tyrone Collins, Eric Pinkard, Demond Williams, Ronnie Green, Richard White and Terry Praylor. They had some good ballplayers at Groveland, probably the best players since Auburn C.F. I enjoyed Groveland – it was nicknamed 'Groovyland,' because it was an easy place to do time. It was also a great facility to lift weights. It had two weight yards and good weights in the gym.

Even though it had plenty of advantages, after being there at Groveland for five years I wanted out. I wanted to go to another facility. It was time to break up that time a little, and time goes faster when you go to a different facility. I asked the captains of the facility to get me transferred. I was tired of Groveland. They moved me across the fence to the Groveland Annex. Before I was moved to the Annex I stole a guy's weapon. Most of the Spanish guys were terrible fighters, so they used a weapon known as a razor or a banger, terms used for a long piece of metal that looked like an icepick. Shoty had it hid in the shower curtain rod, and I took it and gave it to the Muslim community. After I gave it to the Muslims they returned it to Shoty and told him I took it. I heard that he was after me because I had taken his banger.

I was in the Annex part of Groveland for approximately six months before I returned to the main part of the Groveland population. When I returned to the main facility I saw Shoty, and he asked me to come behind a building because he said he wanted to talk to me. I went, knowing he had a weapon on him, but little did he know I had one bigger than his. So when he pulled his out, I pulled mine out. He froze and walked away. The Annex was very small and quiet, and I stayed there for just a few months before getting tired of that place. I asked them again to ship me out, but they wouldn't do it. They said I had to do something that would place me in isolation for more than seventy-five days.

So, I started writing bogus grievances, thinking maybe that would get me out. Then I began fighting. I had about four fights in 2001. I didn't care anymore. Some of the younger guys liked to watch BET raps – every day. It came on at the same time as the local and world news, and I tried to watch the news at least twice a week. We agreed on a system, to take turns. One day it was our turn to watch the news and one of them wanted to watch BET raps, and we argued. I changed the channel to the news, he changed it back to BET raps, and when I reached to change it again, I got punched. He pushed me back over some chairs. I looked up and he was sitting on my chest, about to punch again. I was able to wrestle him off, then I got on top and beat his ass. I only hit him three times and my friends stopped the fight. I was mad and I asked them why they stopped me, because I wasn't finished. They said I was hitting him too hard, and I may have killed him if they allowed me to continue. I was

Lu Martin

MILK, Lower Right, best player I ever played along side

Remembering the

Life of…

Robert Todd Echols

Sunrise
October 23, 1962

Sunset
April 29, 2017

Todd Echols Memorial Service

full of anger and rage then, plus I was working out hard. I weighed about 230, solid.

There were two guys there at Groveland who were really good ballplayers — one was name X and the other Q. They were both 'God Bodies,' or "Five Percenters,' a religious group within the prison. They were the best players in Groveland. I would always brag that I was the best in Groveland, because when my team would play theirs, they would switch off guarding me. I was honored. They have both since passed. X (Lu Martin), was from Niagara Falls and Q (Todd Echols) was from Rochester. Lu (X) died in a car accident in 2016 and Q got shot at a Rochester summer league basketball game in 2017. Sad . . . Lu Martin and Milk were both NBA material.

I finally left Groveland in 2001. Before leaving I had about four fights, and I accumulated about 10 tickets — Tier I, II and III. Tickets are like misbehavior reports, given for things you do wrong in prison. You receive different punishments depending on how serious the offense is and how many you have already accumulated. My last ticket was a Tier III, for that fight I had over the television when that inmate wanted to watch BET raps again and again. I received 90 days in the box, and I even tried to fight in the box. When we were in isolation, we received one hour of recreation per day. There were cages in recreation, and sometimes the COs would put two guys to a cage. There was a guy who was a Blood leader; he was tough when he was in population with his team of about 50 other guys. I remember him eyeballing me, trying to intimidate me. Most of the gang leaders or members are tough when they are around the others, but they're punks when they're alone. So, when I saw him I across the hall in his cell in isolation, I asked him if there was a problem, because he used to look at me a certain way in population. He had nothing to say – punk. I said if he had a problem with me, all he had to do was go to recreation and maybe the COs would place us in the same cage. The punk was quiet after that and never went to recreation. In prison there were some COs who would allow guys time to fight. If both inmates went to the right CO and said they wanted to fight, some would allow it as long as no weapons were used. I did that later in my bid. I had a lot of bitterness bottled up, and fighting was one way I let it out. I had a fake and a straight right-hand punch, and when I landed it my opponent had a hard time recovering. Before he recovered there was another straight right to follow. No one recovered from my two rights.

Leaving Groveland Correctional Facility in 2001 after spending two months in isolation. I was shipped to what they called the S.H.U., or Special Housing Unit, AKA the Box 2000. It was something new in the system — certain facilities had them. These prisoners were the most troubling inmates, the ones who were sent to do their isolation time in months or years. For my time in S.H.U., I was shipped to Gouverneur Correctional Facility. Gouverneur is located in St. Lawrence County, in a town where there is also a huge Army base called Fort Drum. It was a new facility built just for housing the most troubling inmates, and it held well over 2,500 prisoners. The worst part of it is the fact that it was built for two inmates per cell. Most guys were afraid to be housed in isolation with another person they did not know, and guys were tested in those cells. Take my advice – if you cannot fight, do not go to S.H.U. Most guys were tried and tested.

I was housed with a guy from Buffalo who snored. I would wake him up and ask him to stop. He tried to get tough with me; he was same height but heavier than me. Most guys will get tough right up until the first punch is thrown and bitch up. I was a seasoned vet and knew how to fight in a six-by-nine cell. He contacted the CO and said he couldn't sleep because I kept waking him up. They moved him out and I was alone for a bit. Then they moved in a young kid who masturbated every morning to the female officer. As long as he did not bother me or do it in front of me, I didn't care. I was in that box for about another two months before getting out before I had to serve my remaining two months of box time.

In approximately 2002, I went to a medium facility in that same county called Riverview Correctional Facility. It was another small and quiet facility. I was very close to the Canadian border in Ogdensburg, N.Y., in St. Lawrence County. You could actually see Canada on a clear day. I wanted to continue my computer drafting classes, but they did not have that program. Another prison facility, Ogdensburg C.F., was just up the road and had drafting. If you have a request and a history in doing a certain job or program, you could request the facility that had your requested program. I requested Ogdensburg and was refused. I acted out, and I was shipped out. While I was at Riverview, I had to go to court to decide if when I was released, was I going to be a level I, II, or III sex offender. I traveled that long transfer back to Ontario County and faced the same judge that sentenced me, who was known to be a tough judge. Not good. He had been a state assemblyman before, and I had written him letters asking for assistance. I had written him several times during my prison term, and he had responded, which made it illegal for him to now handle my sex offender leveling case. But he handled the case anyway.

My attorney for my sex offender leveling was a guy I went to high school with, Alan Reed. He was very good, but the judge was having none of it. According to the sex offender assessment form technically and legally I was to be a level II sex offender, but the judge made me a level III. Being a Level I, II, or III sex offender depends on a number scale. Did the crime happen at night? Were there one or two victims? Weapon? Age? etc. I was in Ontario County just for that hearing. The traveling from St. Lawrence County down to Ontario County was a huge pain. I had to make that long bus ride with about 100 other guys, shackled hands and feet to another person. God forbid if you had to go 'number two'. That long journey back to Ontario County began at a facility called Upstate Correctional which was further north in Franklin County. Upstate Correctional was a transit facility, just like

Downstate Correctional Facility. From there it was a l-o-n-g ride to Downstate Correctional Facility, a four-day trip with umpteen stops. After facing the judge I knew he was not going to give me the Level II. He added points to the sex offender assessment sheet that made me a Level III. I got back to Riverview Correctional four days later. What a pain.

When we were in that area we always drove down highway 5 and highway 20 — shackled, very close to my home. I had been back in Riverview for about a month deciding if I was to be a level II or III sex offender. I knew damn well the judge was not going to give me level II, so I refused to go back to court. Plus, I did not want to travel for four days, eating bagged lunches, shackled to another guy on a bus full of one hundred other guys, making twenty stops, those shackles so uncomfortable on my legs and wrists. I spoke to my attorney, telling him to do the court hearings without me, and I explained that the judge was not going to give me level II. He agreed.

The judge tried to have me 'physically' brought back to court. He wanted his glory in putting this ordeal in the paper – again. He could not legally get me physically brought back, so the case was held without me and of course I was given Level III. During my sentencing times I always wondered if the wives of the attorneys, D.As, or judges ever got involved in cases. For example, I have wondered, how did the judges' wives feel about the time their husbands gave me? Did they feel sad or happy? Justifiable? Did they see a pattern in their husbands' decisions? The Honorable Fred Reed was nice and fair, and I had tried to get him for my sex offender leveling but the judge wanted to sentence me. Judge Reed was well-liked. I never wondered how his wife felt, because he was a fair judge.

In 2002 I was sent back to Elmira Correctional Facility, this time as a population prisoner. Elmira C.F. was run like a real prison. It was very old, with old cells and gates. The COs there were hard and did not play. My program there was drafting, a program I really enjoyed. On July 8, 2003, when we were let out for programs, a different alarm went off. This was an alarm that I had never heard before. Usually we would hear a horn that would indicate five minutes before the gates opened for programs. This alarm was different. It was an alarm for escaped inmates. The prison was in lockdown. We had televisions in our cells, and the Elmira news stated that two inmates had escaped from the Elmira State Correctional Facility. Down the unit, you could hear guys cheering. The prison was in lockdown for approximately three days, meaning we had to stay in our cells all the time and eat bagged lunches, until we were let out and allowed to go to programs.

Two guys had escaped — both white guys named

Tim. I did not really know them, but I remember seeing them in the cafeteria line at chow. Everybody was happy for them. The news showed the sheets that they used to get down the side of the prison wall. Their cells were in the same block as I was in — F Block. They had a program that allowed them to get tools, like a sledgehammer and screwdrivers, which they had used to get out through the ventilation duct. After approximately five days on the loose they were caught. When it was announced on the news you could heard everybody moan in sadness. I was on the sixth floor (tier), which had 20 cells per floor. It was all open space. Eventually, I found out that the guy who was supposed to pick the two Tims up that night had been caught for DWI and was in the county jail. If that guy didn't get arrested and sent to jail for that DWI charge, they would have made it out forever. We heard they were given ten years in the box (isolation) and a new charge for escape. They were now lifers.

In my drafting class I was told that there was a guy going around talking about my being a sex offender. I approached him and told him if he mentioned me one more time, I was going to beat his ass. Then I was told that he was still talking about me being a sex offender, so I went to the prison guard, Mr. C., who was in charge of our block. I went to Mr. C. and told him that this guy was going around the facility telling people about my offense. I asked him if I could kick his ass, and he said "Yes, just wait until this afternoon when we are let out for chow." That evening when we were let out for chow, I saw him talking on the phone in the basement. I went up to him smacked the phone out of his hand and face. I punched him more in the face and body. He never had a chance, plus he could not fight. I went to chow and when I came back my cell was set on fire. He had stayed back and thrown lighter fluid in my cell, and 60 percent of my property was gone. When something like that happened, you were immediately taken to Protective Custody (P.C.), AKA Punk City. Prisoners called it punk city because it was where most guys signed themselves in to get out of regular population because they were afraid of someone specific or just afraid of regular population in general.

I was interviewed by a captain I had known from Groveland. I was honest with him and told him that I had beaten the other inmate's ass because he was talking shit about my crime. I asked him if he would let me back into population. He said wasn't supposed to and I knew that, but I convinced him that I needed to get back to population to even a score. He said OK, and he let me back into regular population after about two weeks. Some prison guards did not care if inmates hurt, cut or stabbed each other. I was finally let back, and when I walked into the chow hall and I could see most of the population turn and look at me. They were probably wondering if I was going to set if off (start fighting) right there in the chow hall with at least 1,000 guys in there. I was not.

I saw the guy who torched my cell and yelled to him that revenge was coming as soon as I could catch him in the right place. He said he did not do it. I told him he was a liar and that his ass was mine. The Latin Kings came to me and told me he had offered them $300 to cut me and get me out of the facility. He had no idea the leader liked and respected me. He told me that he was going to collect the $300 and cut him instead. Word got back to him about their plan, and he signed into Protective Custody and was shipped out of the facility. I filed a claim for my personal items being torched, and after my release I went to small claims court in Binghamton and was awarded $750 for my items. The only thing that was not replaceable was a small photo album I had with pictures of my then-girlfriend. I honestly believe the CO that searched my cell after the fire purposely threw that photo album out. She was a very beautiful white girl, and prison guards did not like seeing pretty white girls coming to visit black inmates, nor did they like seeing photos of white girls. That was the only photo album that was missing.

During my prison days I wrote some small poetry, which helped me process what I was going through and express my emotions.

Listen

By Bronson Frank

I want to send a message to young people who are free
This is an urgent message so you don't end up like me

For I have lost my freedom, I'm locked inside a steel cage
Where there's no sunshine or joy, only bitterness, regret and rage

I've only painful memories of the life and love I lost
I played the game – made my mistakes and now I'm paying the cost

So listen carefully to my warning – stay far from drugs and crime!
Or you may wake up some morning in a cage of steel – doing time!

Behind the Wall
By Bronson Frank

It's a most unusual city behind the wall
Concrete jungle, large but small

Filled with people from everywhere
Crimes they committed got them there

Smugglers, thuggers, killers and thieves
Living in a jungle without any trees

Once you're inside it's a whole new story
The games people play are just for glory

Killing and stabbing most every day
It's all just part of the penitentiary way

They use words and phrases that you don't understand
But here in the jungle it's the tongue of the land

So you had a family, a friend, a wife or a girl
Hearing from them puts you in a whirl
Wanting to be back in the real world.

Holes in Time

By Bronson Frank

Time goes by, days, weeks and years
While down my cheeks fall many tears

I miss my family that I've brought to shame
I could not win at Satan's game

The crooked dealer filled our hearts with pain
I wonder will it pass or will it remain

Can time fill the hole so deep and wide
Or will it sweep us under like an ocean tide

Our heads are bent like a weeping willow
And sleepless nights on a tear soaked pillow

I've nothing to do but end this rhyme
And return to filling holes in time

BRONSON

A Taste of Freedom

When my mom passed in December 1991, I remember one of the top leaders in the facility came to my cell and asked if I was OK. His name was Al Lopez, and he was the most respected Hispanic in the entire facility. He had at least 1,000 guys at his command. He was a top leader. For him to come to my cell to check on me meant a lot. He and I sat and talked, and he made tuna fish sandwiches for us both. Just to be seen talking to Al was a big plus for me. I went home for my mom's funeral; she looked beautiful. I was escorted to her funeral by one of the Moribitos, a correctional officer at Auburn. The funeral home, Palmisano's, did a good job on her. She looked at peace. She passed of uterine cancer, in three months. I was thankful I was able to talk to her and apologize for my stupid crimes. She asked me to find out why I committed those crimes and to get into therapy. I did, and therapy was the best thing I ever did. (Therapy works). Telling these stories about my parents passing away brings sadness and a thankful smile.

My dad passed on August 30, 1969. He was raised in Dresden-Jerusalem, N.Y. He was employed by the Bouley Construction Company as a mason foreman. He was a member of Trinity Church and member of Bricklayers, Masons and Plasterers International Union 43, and also a member of Winnek Post American Legion because he served in World War II. When my dad passed when I was only twelve years old, I woke to screaming from my mom. My dad was a construction worker; he stood 6-foot-5. He was an outdoorsman.

Funeral Service For
Marie F. Frank
1924 - 1991

Tuesday, December 17, 1991 12 p.m.
Mt. Olive Church
70 Clark Street, Geneva, NY
Rev. E. Johnson, Pastor

He liked to hunt, fish and trap game. He usually took us kids with him. He was raised in the Penn Yan-Jerusalem, New York area, and he also came from a large family. He passed away from cancer. He was sick for approximately six months before he came home – to pass. He came home from the hospital in Buffalo and went to the Geneva General Hospital. He was home for about a month before he passed. When my younger sister Brenda woke me and told me he passed, I laid in bed for a while and finally forced myself out of bed. I went downstairs to everybody crying.

My neighbor Ricky James asked me to go for a walk to get away from it all. We began walking down Middle Street, and a man named Junior Yancey stopped and gave us a ride. We got in and he said to me, "I hear your dad passed." I didn't know what to say. He then said, "I'm sorry to hear that." Those kind words stuck with me through all these years, and they meant a lot. Every time I think of losing my dad I think of that

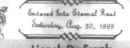

Entered Into Eternal Rest
Saturday, Aug. 30, 1969

Lionel D. Frank

GENEVA — Lionel D. (Lee) Frank, 53, of 68 Evans St., died Saturday in Geneva General Hospital, following an extended illness.

Funeral services will be at 11 a.m. Wednesday in Trinity Episcopal Church with the Rev. Dr. Richard Day, officiating. Burial will be in Glenwood Cemetery.

Friends may call at the Corwin Funeral home this afternoon and evening.

Mr. Frank was born in Dresden and had been a resident of Geneva for more than 30 years. He was employed with the Bouley Construction Co. of Auburn as a mason foreman.

He was a member of Trinity Church, and a member of the Bricklayers, Masons and Plasterers International Union Local 45, and also a member of Winnek Post American Legion, having served in World War II.

He is survived by his wife, Marie; four daughters, Mrs. Barbara VanAlstyne, Bonita, Beth and Brenda all of Geneva; four sons, Lionel Jr. (Butch) U. S. Army stationed in Hawaii, Barron, Bronson, and Brian all of Geneva; his mother, Mrs. Eva Hoskins of Dresden; three granddaughters; four sisters, Mrs. Inez Sheppard of Elmira, Mrs. Alice Reed of Elmira, Mrs. Leola Thomas of Niagra Falls, and Mrs. Eva Moody of Oakland, Calif., and two brothers, Robert of Stanley and Francis of Lockport; and several nieces and nephews.

Lionel D. Frank Obituary

Lionel D. Frank

45

kind man with those kind words. I carried those kind words from Mr. Yancey for many years. At the age of 60 I finally decided to meet this man and thank him. My friend Larry Mallard took me to his house in Geneva and reminded him of that August day in 1969, telling him about how his kind words carried me throughout all these years. It was a good feeling to finally meet him.

When my mom passed, I was at the Auburn Correctional Facility. My sister Barbara and her husband David came to visit, and I could tell by the looks on their faces that something sad had happened. They then told me my mom had passed. I was always thankful for the time I had spent with her before she passed. After that visit I headed back to my cell, and as I turned the corner I saw several guys standing in front of my cell. They said they heard I had a passing in my family and were sorry to hear that and asked if was there was anything they could do to help. I said, "No, I'm fine." The others left, but Al stayed to talk and eat tuna sandwiches. So, I will always remember when both my parents passed there were two very nice people on both those days to help me get through it. Thank God for them.

In September 2005 I was (allegedly) released from incarceration at the Mid-State Correctional Facility. I was geared to come home. I went to the parole counselor and signed the papers for release. The parole counselor

Manhattan Psychiatric Center

said, "Congratulations, you are going home." And then her phone rang. She answered, and the look on her face was not good. She hung up and told me it was the senior parole officer in Monroe County, and he wanted me to call him back after I left that office. I told her, "That does not sound good." She assured me that I had just signed the release papers and I was going home. I went back to my housing unit and was told to return to the parole office. I walked in, and again the look on her face told it all. She apologized and said she is not sure what was going on, but I would not be going home; instead I would be going to the Manhattan Psychiatric Center in New York City for some minor evaluations before I could be released.

At first, I refused to re-sign other papers to go to a different facility when I had just signed papers for home. After arguing with my parole counselor, she finally convinced me to sign the new papers. I signed and was taken to the Box for some reason. I was stripped of my clothes and only given a sheet and the mattress to lay on. I was not allowed to call my family, who would be waiting for me at the bus station. The next morning I was taken to the Manhattan Psychiatric Center in Harlem. I was initially told that I would be there a few days for an evaluation. However, the folks at the Psychiatric Center told me otherwise. I was going to be there for much longer. I was taken to a ward on the ninth floor where I was being housed with other sex offenders who were brought there the same way I was. They were also due to get out but instead brought there by the state.

We were told that Governor Pataki had just began a new law that was called the Civil Confinement Law. There were approximately 30 of us. We were bamboozled. I was there until July 2007, for almost two years. The workers there were as surprised as we were. Most of them were very nice. Some of the girls there liked me and brought me some of their boyfriends' clothes. Plus, there were other things going on for me with them…I had not had sex in approximately 20 years so the first few times I tried to have sex, I was too nervous. They were more than willing. I was afraid that these girls were trying to set me up. After they convinced me they were not undercover police, they brought in condoms for me and we went into a

closet in the laundry room. And we began having sex in my room. I had a room to myself. They checked my doctor's records and saw I did not have a disease and they brought papers to show they did not have any type of disease. So then we began having unprotected sex. To this day I am still in contact with some of them. When I was at the Manhattan Psychiatric Center my friend Teresa Javarone from Gloversville, N.Y. sent me a card to pray with Saint Jude. It was a three-by-four card, and on the back it had a prayer to pray in hopeless situations. She asked me to read that prayer, and I did. The next morning, I was told I was getting released. On that card it states that I promise not to forget Saint Jude for this great favor. And I have not. I have a tattoo that says "Saint Jude' on my abdomen.

I was finally released from The Manhattan Psychiatric Center in July of 2007. I was probably the eighth sex offender to be released. We had independent attorneys fighting for us, and we were slowly being released. I said goodbye to the nice people that worked there. The other sex offenders were not really happy that they were staying, but people were being released weekly. I knew how they felt, because I saw approximately seven guys leave before me. I was not friends with the entire staff. I had some smartass comments for some of them before I left. I rubbed it in the face of some of the guys who worked there that I was getting more sex than they were.

That morning I was escorted by four staff members to the NYC Port Authority Terminal on 42nd and 7th Avenues. I was in shackles. I got to the bus and there was a very long line for the bus I was to take. One of the escorts I was with boarded the bus and told the Greyhound bus driver that he had a person that had to be boarded. He told him that I was being released from imprisonment at the Manhattan Psychiatric Center and I was to go to Rochester. The bus driver made room for me on the bus. I sat alone. When I got onto the bus, still shackled, I could hear the conversations on the entire bus stop, and everyone turned to look at me being escorted and placed in a seat. I said my goodbyes to the staff who escorted me. Being FREE for the time being felt good, scary, strange, and exciting. Seeing the many sites that as a prisoner I had not seen in decades was amazing. I was looking out the window and taking in all the new-old familiar sites. The cars, the trees, the houses, the clothes people were wearing, people on cell phones, the colors, the smells – it was a new world.

Approximately halfway to Rochester, we stopped in Syracuse at a Burger King. I was afraid to get off the bus. One of the bus drivers saw that I was not getting off and asked if I was OK. He said he knew about my long 20-year ordeal of incarceration and assured me that I would be safe getting off the bus and going into Burger King. I forced myself off the bus, even though I was afraid. I began breathing heavily, and everything began to get hot. I was hyperventilating. I had to stop walking. The bus driver came to me again and asked if I was OK, and I said yes, even though my heart was racing. I got in line and ordered a burger, fries and a drink. The order came and she placed the bag down with an empty cup. I thought maybe she had forgotten to place the soda in the cup. I looked at the cup and then back at her like, "Where is the soda?" She said, "Sir, you can get the soda over there at the soda fountains." I felt shamed and embarrassed. Before my imprisonment, they had brought the soda in the cup. Things had changed – now you got the cup and it was self-serve. I sat and ate what I could, but I was still very nervous.

Everyone was getting back on the bus. I finished and took my trash to the bin, and I saw a cell phone sitting there. I dared not touch it, feeling I was being set up. I told the bus driver who had been watching me, and he got it and asked if anyone had left a cell phone in the restaurant. An Asian lady said yes and took it, and the bus driver told her that I had found it. She came over and thanked me. We got back on the bus, and again I started to stare out the window. All the way to Rochester, I couldn't stop looking at the different styles of cars, the clothes, the colors, the smells, the trees, the grass, everything. We stopped once again. I think it was in the Utica area. I again hesitated at getting off, but seeing the bus driver watching me, I got off. When I stepped off the bus, a very tall state trooper was standing there. I froze, and my breathing stopped. After standing still for several seconds I realized he was not going to say anything to me. I forced myself to continue to walk and went inside, went to the bathroom and immediately got back on the bus. We finally arrived at the Rochester bus terminal.

Before leaving the Manhattan Psychiatric Center, I had to write down what I would be wearing, so that I could be identified. I began to get off and saw what looked like an undercover police officer. I saw him look at me and used his fingers to call me over. He asked me my name, and he introduced himself as parole officer Casselman and introduced me to my parole officer, Ms. Sheila Tanea. I immediately recognized the last name, and I wondered if she knew Mike and Tim Tanea from Newark. (It turned out she was related to them.) They took me to the Rochester parole office, where I completed some paperwork. I had heard stories about the senior parole officer there, and he came in and introduced himself as Bill Fortune. He's the guy who had made the phone call to my parole counselor that sent me to the Manhattan Psychiatric Center almost two years prior. He seemed hard, and all the stories I heard about him seemed to be true from the first meeting. P.O. Tanea seemed to be nice. I told her about knowing Mike and Tim Tanea, Chip Blummer, Jeff Peters and my favorite Newark player, Bob Bushart. She said there was always a debate on who was the better player, Mike or Tim Tanea. I said that's an easy decision – Mike.

We finished the paperwork and she and P.O. Casselman took me to my motel room. It was the Budget Inn, on the corner of Route 96 and 332 in Farmington. Ms. Tanea told me about the Cats bus line to use, and then she and P.O. Casselman left. When they were gone, I felt very nervous and afraid again in this new world. Once I was in the hotel room, I finally called my family told them were I was. Before Ms. Tanea left, she had asked me if I had photos of any children under the age of 18. I said yes, I have pictures of my many nieces and nephews. She said I had to get rid of all of them. Instead I gave all of my five photo albums to family members. Some of my family came over to the Budget Inn to visit. It was so great to see my family, but also strange. I had missed them so much but I also felt embarrassed and ashamed.

The next morning I forced myself outside into a new world. There was a CVS on the corner across from my hotel, but when I began walking across Route 332 everything began to get hot again. I was hyperventilating. I froze, turned around in the middle of Route 332, and went back into the room. I could not do it. I stared out the window for hours. I finally got the courage to try again. I again crossed Route 332 to the CVS, and this time I made it. Walking into the store, I noticed the colors were so bright and vibrant. It was like walking into a maze of different colors. I was used to the drab gray and ugly green colors of the prison world. The signs, colors, smells, people and sounds were all foreign to me. I walked through the store quickly, because my breathing was increasing again. I believe I purchased some gum. I got outside and gave a sigh of relief – I did it!!

Back in my room, I watched TV until the next morning, when I had to report to Ms. Tanea at the sheriff's office in Canandaigua, which is also where my parole meetings were held. I stayed at that motel for about a week, and then I moved to Canandaigua. I got a room at a boarding house above Attorney Schuppenour's Office on Main Street, above Patti's Diner. It was dirty, but it was far better than where I had been over the past 20 years. There were approximately six other parolees on that floor and another eight on the first floor. We all shared one kitchen, bathroom, shower, and toilet. Again, it was 1,000 times better than that six-by-nine cell I had lived in for 20 years. I began going to the Canandaigua Veterans Administration as part of a CWT (Comprehensive Work Therapy) program. I escorted the veterans to and from their scheduled appointments. I believe it was $1 per hour.

I also started going a gym in Canandaigua called Uptown Fitness. I had money from the Manhattan Psychiatric Center, and I went there almost every day. Being in the gym working out brought me comfort. I would be in there for three hours at a time, easy. Sometimes I would go back twice a day. One day the owner, Mr. Ralph Gullace, saw me com-

My first boarding house

ing in for the second time that day and said, "Wow, you must like it here!" I said I did, and I proceeded to go in and work out. I was kind of embarrassed, but the gym was my refuge. I remember having old headphones and a big CD player, while everyone else had mp3 players. I was embarrassed, but it was all I had. Mr. Gullace and his son Matt later came to be very close friends. I had

Second boarding house

Third boarding house

no idea that Mr. Gullace had known who I was, that I was the sex offender who had just returned home to Ontario County. Apparently I was in the newspapers – on the front page. He later told me that he knew who I was. A schoolteacher whose husband worked there had also recognized me, and Mr. Gullace said that some people had complained about me being there. He said he told them that as long as I paid my membership, placed the weights back as I found them, and did not cause any problems, I was welcome there just like anyone else. I appreciated that.

I moved up from the CWT program at the Canandaigua VA to another program, where I worked in the laundry/linen department. I applied for a full-time position and got hired. I believe I got that full-time position because of a guy who was the assistant director at the VA, Mr. Crougar. He was from Penn Yan, and I first met him around 1974 when I was a 4-H camp counselor and he was the camp director. I was doing very well at the Canandaigua VA. I moved to a much better rooming house on Bristol Street. The owner was a guy named

Fourth and last boarding house

Billy Houle. I was finally getting used to walking down the streets. I met a girl who I used to see at parole. Her name was Katie Ayers. She was recently released from incarceration also, and we exchanged phone numbers and decided to meet.

Being on parole, you are not to associate with another parolee on the outside. She would sneak over to my place on Bristol on Tuesdays, because we knew that those were the days the parole officers were meeting their parolees in Geneva. She would come over and we would talk and I began having feelings for her. We dated for a short time. We are still in touch to this day.

I also met a very beautiful girl named Liz Gemili. It was around 2008, and I met her at Eastview Mall, She was

a mix of Mexican and Italian and extremely beautiful, so I decided to try and speak with her. I started a conversation about the coffee she had just purchased from Barbra Jeans coffee shop. I was very nervous, but she gave me her phone number and we later met and started dating. She would come over and stay the night on weekends. I enjoyed her. After being with Liz for a month or so I decided I should tell her about my past, my crime and my many years of imprisonment. She later said she was not afraid of me because of how she had

Liz, me, and Sandra

Liz

grown to like me. She accepted me, and we continued. I realized that telling someone of my past in the beginning is not a good idea. I wanted people to get to know ME first before I told them. I found that if I tell females in the beginning about my offense, I'm finished.

I later met a girl named Barb Briggs. She also worked out at Uptown Fitness. We exchanged numbers at the gym and met for coffee at the Sheraton Restaurant on Main Street. After the third or fourth time we met, I decided to tell her about my crime and my past and prison time. After that meeting I did not hear from her for several weeks. I knew she needed time to process what I had told her, or she would not call me back. She finally did and she said she appreciated me telling her. I hear from her once in a while. We are friends to this day. She is a very nice person and dresses well. Her grandma would always kid her about being all "gussied up."

I also met a girl at the Canandaigua VA named Laura Parker-Shaugnessy. I went through the same routine, with not telling her in the first few weeks and then telling her about my past. She accepted me, and we began seeing each other. It was her walk that attracted me to her. It was a walk that meant business. I nicknamed her "The Walker." She worked on 3A ward. After being friends with her for months, she came to me that she had heard that some people I knew from home was saying some not-nice things about me and my past. It was just one of the many times my own black people talked bad about me. I have to honestly say that when I came home from 20 years of incarceration, white people did more for me than the blacks. Sad but true. A black lady Ms. S. Reed said not so nice things about me at the V.A. and a Black girl Denise Parker-Cunningham, I once dated, called the police on me and then called my Parole Officer - while I was working near her home.

A New World

I remember when I came home, I was used to covering the toilet with toilet paper before sitting down. I was used to wearing my underpants in the shower; it was a respect thing not to show your genitals while in the shower room with up to thirty guys. I was also still wearing shower shoes in the shower. I had to get used to getting in the shower without shower shoes. I continued to use a plastic soap dish. I remember when I first sat on my own toilet seat, it felt funny, but I got used to it. I also remember getting in my shower with my underwear still on. I finally got used to taking a shower naked. In prison, I was also used to wearing a cover over my eyes while I slept. I used to sew a sock together and wear it over my eyes. I did that for a while after coming home, and I also used to roll toilet paper in my ears to keep the noise out. I continued to wear toilet paper in my ears for years.

I remember eating ramen noodles so often that to this day I have not eaten one. Another thing I stopped eating was peanut butter and jelly sandwiches — none to this day. I remember the first time I went into a larger store – Top's in Canandaigua. I first noticed the bright colors, signs, the clean smell and the people's clothes. I went into the aisle that had cereal and I could not believe all of the different varieties. Before I went to prison there were probably two shelves of different cereals, and now there was an entire aisle. My next big store was the Walmart in Canandaigua, and on that shopping trip I began hyperventilating and had to step outside for a few minutes.

There was a very nice man in Canandaigua named Mr. Dick Hill, and he would help people who were recently released from incarceration. He would come and pick me up with several other guys and take us to church. There was a church in Canandaigua on North Road called Canandaigua Baptist Church, which is now the Life Springs Church. I attended that church, and that is where I met my 'Earth Angel' Sandra Snyder. I had been going there for a month or so, and I continued to see a very beautiful white lady there. She had beautiful white hair. She was in charge of greeting the new people and gathering information. She approached me one day for my information, and I was hesitant to tell her that I was recently released from incarceration for a sex offense.

But I did. Being the true Christian that she is, she accepted my telling her. (She has been my very best friend ever since that day in 2008). We became friends, we started working out at the Uptown Fitness gym. She brought me to her home in Bloomfield, and I took her to Geneva and introduced her to my family. I also took her to my home church, which is the Mount Olive Missionary Baptist

Me and Sandra Snyder

Church in Geneva, and she later became a member there. We are going on our 14th anniversary of being best friends. I believe Sandra is heaven-sent.

Sandra was sixty-eight when we met, and it has been fourteen years of being very best friends. After we became friends, I introduced her to my world and she introduced me to hers. I always tell people Sandra is my Earth Angel. I truly believe God gave me Sandy to help me on this journey. I love being with Sandra. People always give her compliments on her hair. She has beautiful white hair. I have always said if it were not for Sandra, I would not have half of what I have today. Sandra wants to move to North Carolina. She is a country person and she will be looking for a country-style home.

I remember taking her to my room that was above Attorney Schuppenhauer's office. I felt ashamed; it was dirty and small. She took me to her house. We began going to the gym at Uptown Fitness. It has been 14 years since we have been best friends. People see us together and think we're a couple. In a sense, I guess we are. However, we are not intimate. Sandy believes the age difference is a problem; I do not. I cannot say it enough that if it were not for Sandy I would not have half of what I have today. I thank God for Sandy. Sandy likes to go go go and I like to nap nap nap. There have been times that we would go to the gym for hours, and then she would come home and mow the lawn. I was tired from the gym and wanted to eat and rest, and she wanted to mow her one acre of land.

One day Sandra and I were at Walmart, and we were seen by one of the deacons of that church. The next time I came to that church I was told by Mr. Dick Hill that the other deacons of that church wanted to set a rule for me stating that I was not allowed to be friends with any church members outside of church. I did not agree with that, and neither did Mr. Hill nor Sandra. I stopped going to that church, along with Mr. Hill and Sandra. I then met another man, Glen Feidner, who took us newly released guys to church at the Calvary Chapel of the Finger Lakes on Route 332. That church wanted us released inmates to use a side door instead of the front door, and we all had to sit together in the front of

Pilgrim Holiness Church

the church. So I decided not to attend that church, which seemed to go against the idea of WWJD. I then went to another church in Canandaigua called the Pilgrim Holiness Church with my landlord Hugh VanNorman. They recognized me from being in the paper, and after my first visit they told Hugh that I was not welcomed at that church and not to bring me back. So I was striking out with churches.

I started volunteering at the food banks in Canandaigua. There was one at the First Congregational Church on Main Street, and I went in and visited with the pastor. I told him about my recent release from incarceration and said that I wished to volunteer for his food pantry, so that I could give back. He seemed like a nice guy but quickly reported me to my parole officer, saying he thought I wanted to be a part of his volunteer program to get closer to the youth. That was the furthest thing from the truth. These lessons taught me that not all churchgoing people live by the Bible.

December 1, 2008 marked a low point for me. I was employed full-time at the Canandaigua Veterans Administration and about to start a part-time job at Walmart. One night seven parole officers came to my room to search. They checked my cell phone and saw that Katie Ayers and I had been text messaging each other, and I was taken into custody. I lost my job at the Canandaigua VA and was given one-and-a-half years back in prison. Katie received nothing.

Going back to prison was very hurtful and embarrassing. Those eighteen months were far worse than the prior 20 years I had completed. Getting a taste of freedom and then going back to prison hurt twice as bad. My parole officer Ms. Tanea requested that I get two years, and I did one-and-a-half years at the Wyoming Correctional Facility. It was a small medium-security facility in Wyoming County. Sandy came to visit me almost every weekend. I did not like the idea of her coming to visit me so often, but she insisted. She's precious.

In 2010, after I was released from that parole violation, I came back home to Canandaigua. I moved into a much better rooming house than the one on Bristol Street — at 32 Chapin Street. It was owned by Hugh and Mary VanNorman. The city of Canandaigua began to give

Hugh and Mary a hard time about who they were renting to, and they had to sell several of their houses. I had 2 roommates, and it was a very nice living situation. While living on Chapin Street, Phil Meek, his wife Megan and two children, son Caleb and daughter Sylvia, lived next door. Their son Caleb was very young. After coming home from 22 years of incarceration, hearing baby Caleb cry was music to my ears. I used to sit listening to him cry. I hadn't heard a baby cry in 22 years, and it was a beautiful sound. One day I saw Phil outside and introduced myself. I told him about my crime and that

Bill Thomas

I was recently released from 22 years of incarceration. I essentially explained to him that he had no reason to be afraid and that I would not be a threat to him and his family. A month or so later he thanked me for coming to him and said he believed me and the words I spoke. He said that I seemed sincere in what I had told him. I asked him to thank his son for that beautiful sound. It truly calmed me. Their daughter Sylvia liked releasing my White Birds. Phil said he enjoyed my book and this has encouraged him to read more books.

Miscellaneous Freestylin': Bill Thomas was a man that my mom began dating in 1973. He was a captain in the Army who was stationed at the Seneca Army Depot. He was a nice man, more like a friend to us kids. We naturally gave him a hard time at first, but he soon won us over. He passed in 1990 from cancer. He lost his voice box. He was a great man.

When I played high school basketball our point guard was Bob McLane. He was a good ball handler and

excellent shooter. When I was at Auburn C.F. 1991 he came to visit me and I appreciated that visit. Then when I was at Elmira C.F. 2003, we had been corresponding. He was nice enough to send me some sweatpants and hoodies, again I appreciated that. I worked at the American Can with his dad and I used to

Mark Pitifer's book cover

go to his home on Washington Street and shoot baskets. He has a brother Mike and sister Sue. I never met his mom and sure she is a nice lady. He asked me to contact him whenever I got home, so I did. When I came home in 2007, I wrote a letter to his place of business, I also went to his business that's in Farmington and asked the receptionist to ask Bob to contact me and that I was home.

I left my number and address. After several attempts, I gave up realizing that he wasn't interested. It struck me because he had been in contact with me my entire incarceration. I have my thoughts as to why he ignored my attempts in contacting him but I'll leave it alone.

Theresa Pennetta

I would also like to mention Mark Pitifer — a kid everyone who grew up in the Geneva area knows. Being a white man, he likes to brag about how many years he was a park leader in Chartres Homes, overseeing all of the kids in the projects. I think he served as a leader for

Kathy DeJohn-Pierce

fifteen years, and that's a lot of years dealing with black kids, being the only white man in a housing project that's mostly black. I first met Mark when he was helping out on the basketball team at GHS for the 1974-'75 season. He recently asked me if I remember him giving me gum before the games. I (vaguely) remember that. He said his family was poor and he used to save his money to buy me gum from Kay's corner store.

The first good thing about Mark were his parents. Both Mr. and Mrs. Pitifer were very nice people. Mark's sisters were Sally, Shari and Charla. I first met Sally and Shari back when I was a camp counselor at the 4-H camp in Canandaigua in 1974. I was a counselor who taught swimming. My senior year of high school in 1975, Sally asked me for my autograph. Shari told me years later that Sally still has that autograph I wrote on a pack of matches. I first met the youngest Pitifer daughter, Charla, at

Kennedy Ann Bucklin

FAIRPORT — Kennedy Ann Bucklin, 21-month-old beloved daughter of John and Jacquie Palmieri Bucklin of Fairport, passed away Monday (May 2, 2005) after a valiant nine-month battle with cancer.

Relatives and friends are invited to call from 3 to 8 p.m. Thursday (May 5) at the Richard H. Keenan Funeral Home, 7501 Pittsford-Palmyra Road, Route 31, Egypt location. A Mass of Christian Burial will be celebrated at 9:30 a.m. Friday (May 6) at St. John of Rochester Roman Catholic Church, 8 Wickford Way at Route 31 in Fairport. Burial will be in Glenwood Cemetery, Route 14 South in Geneva, immediately following Mass.

Me, my niece Sham and my nephew Lee

Vicky Bellis's wedding. We danced to a song, and I saw here again years later at a Geneva summer lacrosse game afterparty. I also met Mark's daughter Nina, another beautiful Pitifer. All the females in his family were beautiful and Mark is not – just kidding. LOL. When I came home from incarceration I went to Area Records on Castle Street looking for music from Sally Pitifer, because when I was away I heard she could sing. I then read an article that said she sounded a bit like the great Aretha Franklin. I recently Google her name and found a very nice video of her singing "Ave Maria," "God is Real" "Mary, Did You Know?" I last saw Shari on TV, acting in soap operas, while I was in prison at Groveland Correctional Facility. The last time I saw her in person, she was working at a store on Copeland and Hamilton Street. I recently connected with Mark Pitifer's son on Linkedin.

Me with my two Nieces Tayln and Kelly

Being into sports, I encountered a lot of cheerleaders. In my opinion, the best cheerleaders were Theresa Pennetta and Kathy DeJohn-Pierce. They were a year ahead of me at GHS, and I remember watching how high they jumped. Wow, they could get up in the air! However, the very best cheerleader was Pamela O'Neil, and I say that because she went the farthest in cheerleading. She was a Buffalo Jill – cheering for the Buffalo Bills. Donna Ward was a very good cheerleader as well and a close friend. Donna was like a female Italian stallion. Michelle DeMattis was very good also. I remember first seeing Michelle compete at a Hobart track meet – she was high jumping.

When I was in prison at the Riverview Correctional Facility. I saw in the paper that Johnnie Bucklin and Jacquie Palmeri's baby had passed away. I felt so bad. I remember I started to cry. I had no idea who this little girl was, but I felt bad for Johnnie and Jacquie. Johnnie has a big family who grew up on the corner of Washington and Nagel Street — Patty, Suzanne, Gary, Bobby, Jimmy, Michael and Steve. I used to see Suzanne out and would always say hello. I last saw Suzanne at The Holiday, a bar at the end of Exchange Street. I hear she now lives in Albany. We knew each other well.

My niece Sham (aka Shamsincere) asked me to put a passage in my book about her. Sham, like all Frank girls, is beautiful. I first noticed that Sham had talent in the rapping field when she was young and I heard her beatboxing with her cousins Lee, Don'l and Shawn. I used to take them to the Gorge and to the swimming pool in Watkins Glen, the same pool where my dad took us kids back around 1967. Sham has two daughters. She's shy on stage but not in person. She once said she did not want to perform because all those people were staring at her. I wanted to say, "Duh. That's what happens when you are holding the microphone on any stage." She was employed at Walmart and was a senior legislative clerk at city hall in Rochester. I am encouraging her to continue her vision and become the next Cardi B. She also has street smarts.

When I was a high school sophomore in 1973, I locked eyes with a pretty girl named Debbie Puma. I was a little intimidated because she was a Senior. I first remember her meeting me at a bar in Lyons NY called Tom Jones. I was afraid to go inside but she assured me that I'd be okay. It was smoky and my eyes began to burn. She told me that I was coming home with her that night. She took me outside

Debbi Puma

and we got into hearse that belonged to Ronnie Nappie. It was for funeral services. But in the back was a lot of pillows. We made out. I spent time with her several times, but very nervous. Debbie and I recently spoke, she is doing well in Florida.

When I was a junior in high school there was a guy Jerome Williams who graduated years earlier. He used to come back to the school and pick on me. He dated a girl in my class Maureen Tighe, every time she mentioned my name he'd come to the school and threaten mc. Maureen also liked me. So to get back at Jerome, every time he picked on me I'd secretly go out with Maureen. She lived across the street from the Junior High School, I'd call her and ask her to meet me behind the school and we'd make out. That was my way of getting even with him...

In high school I knew a guy named Andy Candidori. He was a pain in my ass, but a good guy and good athlete. He had a brother named Joe. I was friends with a girl named Kim Khoury, I first met her at a young age. Her family owned a store on Routes 5 and 20, and in the '60s my dad would go there and buy his cases of beer. Kim was friendly, and I got to know her more in grade school, junior high and high school. We continued our friendship after high school, and I went to their wedding at the Houghton House. Kim used to call me Shemp, like the guy from the Three Stooges. She liked me, but we never went out. Donna Scalise would always tell me how much Kim liked it when I wore my afro out. My

Anthony Hudson, me, and Allan Hudson

eighth grade girlfriend was a girl named Patty DeJohn. We used to meet behind St. Stephens Church and kiss. There was a little cubby hole behind the school, and we would go in there. We used to talk on the phone a lot. Patty later dated my brother Barron. When talking on the phone with Patty, I'd hear her mom say, "Get the F@#k of that phone!!" I found it hard to believe a parent would say those words to an eighth grade child.

I also dated Rosemary Rodriguez and Shelly Mattice in high school. After high school I dated Sherry Hynick. Sherry used to sneak me into her house when her dad was home. She lived out near Kashong. Ten years later, in 1986, I began working for NYSEG in Lockport New York, and her dad Mr. Hynick was the personnel manager. I used to go out for drinks with some white girls who were my coworkers, and Mr. Hynick brought me into his office and told me that it didn't look good for me to be dating white girls at work. Little did he know that I used to date his daughter Sherry and I had been in his house when he was home. Sherry would sneak me in the house, saying "Walk behind me taking the same steps." I told the white

Pam O'Neil and my brother Brian in their younger years

girls that I worked with what he said and they were upset, saying it was none of his business what employees did after work. Sherry Hynick graduated from high school early; she was in my graduating class of 1975. She went on to attend Cornell University.

I wanted to tell her dad about me and Sherry being in the next room in his house, just to rub it in a bit, but I never did.

Also around 1976 several of us black guys had white girlfriends, and we would all meet out at Janie Brennan's house. She had a huge house with a pool table in the basement out on Slosson Lane. It seemed like her house had at least eight bedrooms. There were about five of us black guys, all with white girlfriends, and we would meet there for the night. Janie is now married to a good friend of mine, Mike Maher from Waterloo. We would also meet at Carol Kuusisto's house on Main and St. Clair Street. Her dad was a big shot at Hobart. That was another huge house with approximately eight bedrooms.

76

I later saw Carol in Brooklyn, New York in around 1985. There is a famous actress from Geneva named Lauren Holly. She is a 1981 graduate of GHS. I first noticed her she was in the Geneva Times in front of the movie theater with some famous guy. I just Instagrammed her, and I wonder if she will respond. Sometimes I worry how they feel about me contacting them. Because of my past, not everyone is happy to hear from me.

I'd also like to mention a dear childhood friend, Anthony Hudson. He is a trumpet player and Hapkido expert, and he now lives in California. He is the nephew of the famous Wilmer Alexander. Anthony plays in a symphony and a reggae group in California. His brother Allen is also a very close friend. Allen now lives in Ohio and continues to wear his Syracuse Orange gear out there, where he gets dirty looks from the Buckeye fans. Allen loved playing basketball, I remember him playing at Gulvin's park wearing a cast on his arm and still killing guys. I'd like to mention a lady named Andrea 'Dee Dee' Augustine; everyone in Geneva knew her. She was bubbly and very nice. She passed away in February 2018. She was always nice and well-respected in the community, not only by the whites but the blacks as well.

I'd like to mention three people: Mrs. Rose Blue, Patty Blue and Ms. Lucille Mallard. These are three people who have good positions within the city of Geneva. I have always questioned why Rose Blue gave up one of the most powerful positions in Geneva. She was the Human Rights Director. I have always wondered why she gave up a position like that? Something strikes me about her resigning from that powerful position. Patty Blue once had the housing position in Geneva and lost it. Lucille recently donated water and Gatorade for my annual event I have at Gulvin Park in Geneva, "Playin' For Brian."

I'd like to take my hat off to Ms. Pam O'Neil. I first met Pam around 1976; she liked my youngest brother Brian. She would call the house whispering, "Is Brian home?" I would start laughing and say, "Pam, why are you whispering?" She said she was under the covers in her bed and she didn't want her parents to hear her. First, Pam is one of nicest, friendliest, most down-to-earth people you would ever meet. She loved everyone. Pam was a blonde-haired blue-eyed beauty. Pam had a very nice sister named Donna; I worked with Donna at the American Can. Pam's sister Donna sadly lost her life in Waterloo to a man who shot her. I searched for him when I was in prison. Donna's husband Allie Gueurri refused to tell me his name. I know he changed his name also. I hate to say what would have happened to him if I had located him. I used to see Pam when she came home to Geneva from Buffalo.

Pam and I were close then. She would call me and say she was coming home for a few days. I said, "OK, let me know when you get home. She'd say, "OK, I have to go and see the kids first." Meaning Donna's kids. That was Pam's number-one priority when she came home to Geneva, to go see Donna's kids first. Pam had the perfect face, with the best, brightest smile you ever saw. Pam went on to become a Buffalo Jill. Everyone wanted to be her friend. Pam was not only beautiful, but she was talented. Getting to that level you don't only have to have the looks – you have to have the talent also. Pam had it. Pam was also in Playboy magazine's February 1984 edition. Pam helped put Geneva, New York on the map. Pam was second to none. I'll say that again – Ms. Pamela O'Neil was second to none.

BRONSON

Inspirations

I decided to play lacrosse during my senior year in 1975. I had never held a lacrosse stick until the day I walked into Mr. Jack McDonald's locker room. We had just finished basketball sectionals at the then-War Memorial. I was nervous; I had been in football and basketball locker rooms, but never a lacrosse locker room. When I walked in, I saw Coach McDonald do a double take at me. Before I had reached my locker to get undressed, I heard Mr. McDonald say in a loud voice, "So, those two skinny basketball players finally showed up, huh?" He meant me and Jerry Kraus; we had both reported late because of basketball sectionals. Everyone in the locker room laughed and for me it broke the ice because I was nervous. It showed me that he saw me and acknowledged me. I appreciated it. I remember saying to myself, "I think I'm gonna like playing for this guy."

They had to show me how to hold the stick and how to catch and throw the ball, but my first impression was right. I LOVED playing for him.

One day Mark Pitifer asked me who my favorite coach was, and I said Mr. McDonald. He said "Who, Jack?" I

Me in my lacrosse uniform

said, "NO. His name is Mr. McDonald." He was a player's coach. He laughed and joked around. Eighty percent of his coaching style was laughing and joking, and it was very effective. I did not start the first game, but I did start the remainder of the season. I ended up making second team defense. Jack

McDonald knew that the best way to teach an athlete a new sport was by making it FUN. I could not wait to get to lacrosse practice. I excelled. I remember senior skip day in 1975. All the seniors skipped school, and I did too. But when it was time for lacrosse practice, I was the first one there and the last to leave. I was not about to miss practice, even though I was the only senior there. Mr. McDonald made me a very good lacrosse player, and he also made me a better athlete. He polished me up. I loved hearing him yell. I could remember in the games, when our team or our opponent would call a time-out. I would run as fast as I could over to him. I wanted to be right in his face. I could remember elbowing guys out of the way in the huddle to get closest to him. You were not going to get between me and Mr. McDonald in the huddles.

I first remember shifting gears for this man at our Seneca Falls game. Right before we were to take the field over there, someone yelled out 'Where's Bronson?' Some people took it as if they were saying they could not see me. I was the only black at the game. It did not bother me, but Mr. McDonald heard it and didn't like it. So he did what all great coaches do. He turned that negative into a positive to get our team fired up to win that game. In one of his many great pregame speeches he said, "If they want to see Bronson, we'll show 'em Bronson." The team cheered and I felt appreciated. I felt he stuck up for me. It showed me that he cared for me. I appreciated that and I immediately thought of ways to pay him back for sticking up for me. I finally decided that I was going to play a good game to repay him. My paying him back was that I was not going to allow my man to score. I played well, we won the game and my man did not score. That was the first time he motivated me to shift to a higher gear.

The second time was a game against Lafayette High School. I had never heard of them, but they had some big-gun attackman. Mr. McDonald came to me before that game laughing, telling me that this attackman was all this and all that. He also convinced me I was better that this guy, even though I had been playing lacrosse for about five weeks and this guy had been playing probably for his entire life. I looked at Mr. McDonald like, *how could that be?* Mr. McDonald saw my puzzled look and said, "You are better than he is because you're bigger and faster and you can probably hit harder than he can. Yes, he has you beat as far as stick-handling skills. However, if you use your skills that he doesn't have, you can outplay him." It sounded good, so I believed him – first because I really liked Mr. McDonald. I played very well against Mr. All Everything from Lafayette High.

The third shift came in the summer of 1977, when I was playing for the Geneva summer league team. Our final game was against East Irondequoit. I started warming up, looked on the sidelines and saw Mr. McDonald. He had not coached any of our regular season games, but he was going to coach our finals game. I was excited and nervous; I wanted to show him how much better I had gotten since high school. Whenever he wanted me to play a big game, he would call me over and coach me before the game began. He came up to me that day and said that they had some big shot attackman home from college, and as a high schooler he scored a bunch of goals on that very field. He said he was just watching the kid, and he thought he wasn't any good. Again, he told me that I was better than my opponent. He made a big deal of the kid's parents being at the game to see their son score all these goals. Mr. McDonald said, "Not today." Mr. McDonald had this line he would always use. He would say, "I want you to go out there and shut him down. Don't give him anything. Let him know you're from Geneva!" Lastly, he would say, "Don't let him make the same move twice. If he slips up and makes the same move twice, I want you to ring his bell. Mr. McDonald liked bell ringers. Tom Patrick was our bell ringer in high school. I liked Mr. McDonald, so I tried to become a bell ringer for him.

Those were the good times. The only bad time came when he asked me to call him by his first name. It was probably 1977 at a Geneva High football game. I saw him and said, "Hello, Mr. McDonald." He said, "You don't have to call me Mr. McDonald. Just call me Jack." I was crushed that he would ask me to do such a thing. But this is who he was. I remember feeling hurt and shame. There was no way I would ever use his first name. I remember laughing it off and walking away. But I was hurt. A few years ago, Mark Pitifer referred to him as Jack. I quickly corrected him and said, "No, his name is Mr. McDonald." Later that year I saw him again, and again I said, "Hello, Mr. McDonald." He said it again: "You don't have to call me Mr. McDonald. Just call me Jack." I finally said, "I'm sorry Mr. McDonald. I don't want to do that." He understood and said, "OK."

I also decided to play lacrosse my final year to play on the same team as Fran Shields and Jerry Kraus. My first lacrosse stick was given to me by a legendary coach, Jerry Schmidt from Hobart College in Geneva. I called Coach Schmidt and told him I wanted to play lacrosse but did not have a stick. He told me to come to his home, and he gave me a wooden defensive lacrosse stick. I was so happy. The May 29, 2018 article in US Lacrosse Magazine spoke about being Black while playing Lacrosse. I definitely was called a Nigger and treated differently by players and a Coach, who I played for while playing for Miller Lacrosse. He embarrassed me several times and asked me to quit but I wouldn't.

1991 (30 Years Ago)

Baron Frank scored 44 points and Tom Schweitz netted 24 points for De-Maria's in a Geneva men's basketball league game against Zotos.

Daena Abbott and Kelly Fuller were named students of the month at Red Jacket High and Middle schools, respectively.

Wayne County's county-wide curbside recy-

I met Lisa in 1985. I moved to New York City that year with a different girl, but a mutual friend named Mary Visco told me that I should call Lisa when I got to the city. I called Lisa after being there a few weeks, and we met for dinner and soon became lovers and friends. I fell in love with Lisa. She was an extremely beautiful

Italian girl. She loved sports and fashion. She had a good job working in the fashion district of NYC. She graduated from the Fashion Institute of Technology. I have always said Lisa was my biggest loss. She was there for me when I went to prison. She supported

Mary Visco

me from September 1988 to February 1991, and it was very painful losing her. If I knew then what I know now I would — should — have married her.

My world was in a tailspin after Lisa broke up with me. It took me about six months before I came out of that spin. Her parents were not supportive of Lisa dating a black man. They threatened to wash their hands of her if she continued. Lisa continued to see me, and I will always respect her for that. She did not hear from her parents for about six months then, they finally realized she was not going to stop dating me. They reached out to her. They then asked to meet me, and I refused. The same year we separated Lisa married a different Black man, and I hear she had two daughters and moved to North Carolina. During some of my dark days in prison, I would think of Lisa telling me, "B, you have two choices — sink or swim." I began swimming…

In 1996 from prison I wrote a letter to the Geneva Sports Hall of Fame recommending Jerry Kraus, Mary Murphy, Fran Shields and Jay Murphy. The following year, 1997, Fran Shields was inducted. Jerry Kraus was inducted the following year, and Jay Murphy was inducted the year after that. Soon the Hall also inducted Mary Murphy, who averaged 19.5 points per game on the varsity basketball squad as a freshman. Need I say more? I hope to one day meet Mary Murphy. The Hall will never, ever, get it right as far as having the best basketball player in Geneva History enshrined. He is my brother, Barron Frank. Barron stood only six feet tall and center jumped in high school, and I remember watching him outjump guys who were six-foot-six. He graduated GHS in 1973, played for Fulton Montgomery Community College and then Elmira College, where he became an All-American. He is the only All-American basketball player who never made it to the Geneva Sports Hall. (Shame).

I'm not saying this because he was my brother, but Barron Frank was the best basketball player in Geneva History. As athletes, we always say that numbers do not lie. Barron Frank's numbers are better than any basketball player in Geneva History. Barron was the first All America to not make it into The Hall. People still to this day talk about how Barron has been slighted by The Hall. We have agreed that if the Hall ever wanted to induct Barron he will refuse. I believe the induction of Joe Augustine is when everyone - the real athletes of Geneva began talking. I had honestly never heard of him. The Hall dropped the ball on the best basketball player in Geneva history and they know it. I look at some of the basketball players in the Hall and they could not have even stepped on the same court as Barron. The best basketball players in the history of Geneva that The Hall passed on were: Barron and Bronson Frank, Gene and Marvin Sapp, James Thomas, Welton Eldridge and Vincent Ray. I did read up on Augustine, his bio looks pretty good, but all the guys who knew him said he wasn't in the same league as Barron. I take nothing from Augustine, Mark Pitifer said he had a nice jumper. These were the best basketball players in Geneva History. They may not have all went to college but they were the best. My coach, James Sonny Wilson, Al Klestinic, Robert Woody, Charles Pinkard, Albert Sellers, Donnie Williams, Harold Cuda Fryer, Herbie and Jasper Woody, Scottie Bynum, Jim Henderson, and Melvin Bonner.

As for me, I am sure my numbers surpass 90 percent of those in the Hall, but because of my criminal history I will not get inducted, which does not break my heart. Ask any basketball player about Barron and Bronson playing and they will tell you that we were tops. Mark Pitifer has asked me to send my sports history in but I don't want to stir anything up. Besides, the real athletes of Geneva know who the best were. A little on my career my high school career was in three sports: Basketball, Football and Lacrosse. I played football until my junior year at Fullback, Middle Linebacker and Special Teams. Basketball starter all years, averaged around 17 points a game. I played my senior year in Lacrosse, never held a Lacrosse stick until that first day reporting to tryouts. I ended up making second team All Star team. In 1975, I went on to Fulton Montgomery Community College, where I ran point guard. I averaged 12 points per game. In 1976, I was chosen to play against a Russian National Team at Monroe Community College. In 1977, while playing lacrosse for Miller Lacrosse, we played against the top colleges in the area: Cornell, Hobart and Syracuse. Our last game was against the USA National team at Hofstra. I drove there with a close friend of mine, Terry Corcoran, who was a four-time All American Attackman for Hobart. That was probably the highlight of my Lacrosse career. I played on numerous basketball teams and played in tournaments throughout the finger lakes. Myself or Barron won't lose sleep over not being in The Hall. Ask any of the Hall Directors about myself or Barron or our younger brother Brain. (Period). My youngest brother Brian was a very good athlete, also. He was an excellent bowler. I recommended another athlete,

Jennifer Robbins, and she was inducted in 2019.

If you look at the list of athletes in the Hall you will see a lot of familiar family names. I was secretly told that the family members of some of the athletes who got in have made contributions to the Hall, and that helped their relatives get in. I believe Dante Reid has the best numbers of all Geneva athletes. He graduated from GHS in 1989, but just his freshman baseball season he averaged .479 – wow. He was drafted out of high school in 1989 by the Toronto Blue Jays and he made the GHS all-star team three times. My nephew Jeffrey Bostic got inducted in 2015. A guy I'll always look up to is Al Klestinec, who was inducted in 2002. Mark Pitifer said that he still votes for Barron, and the others on the voting board get upset with him. I respect Mark for voting for the best athlete, not a political vote like the others. They all know Barron was one of the best in Geneva history, and to overlook him is a slap in the face.

I recently suggested Marc VanArsdale for coaching lacrosse. He recently had his *fourth* player, Pat Spencer at Loyola (Md.), to win the prestigious Tewaaraton Award. He coached a North-South Lacrosse game, spent fifteen seasons at University of Virginia where they won three championships, and he is now coaching the offense for Loyola. Marc is a dear friend and since being here in North Carolina, any time his team plays or scrimmages at Duke or UNC, he leaves tickets for me to attend. I get to talk to him afterwards. Please induct Marc; he's a great coach. I see how he interacts with the players and they listen. The plays he calls are executed to how he drew them out. He is not a political vote.

My Childhood

I was born on February 20, 1956 to Lee and Marie Frank. I was raised near the corner of Middle and Evans Street in Geneva, and from 1977 to 1985 I lived at 25 Elmwood Place with my sister Barbara's family in Geneva. There were four boys and four girls. All of our names began with the letter B — Barbara, Bonita, Beth, Butch, Barron, Bronson, Brenda and Brian. Brian passed away from a drug overdose in 2014 at the age of 52. My parents were well-respected in the community of Geneva. My dad worked construction and my mom worked odd jobs. We were not well-off by any stretch; however, we rarely went without. My older brothers and sisters had moved out, so it was myself, Barron, Brenda, and Brian at home. Our neighbors were Ricky James and the McCoys, who moved next door above Ricky on the corner. There was Lucille McCoy, Homer, A.J., Joe, Joyce, and

My parents, Lee and Marie Frank

I'm the baby on the bottom right in this one.

Ricky. Ricky James and his mom lived on the first floor of the corner house, and on the other side were Junior and Pearl Mimms. Hattie and Bobby Green were their parents. Junior sadly recently passed of cancer. Next door to them were the Youngers — Kenny, Gregory and Sherry. They adopted Becky Brodie later. Next to them, on the corner of Andes and Evans, was the Taney family. Mr. and Mrs. Cornelius Taney were older folks. I remember their kids coming to visit them. One of his children was Robert Taney, who has since passed away. I last saw him at a DeSales men's basketball tournament that his son Robert was playing in.

I remember the day Mr. Cornelius Taney died when we were young. We noticed how quiet it was the day of his funeral. No birds were chirping on Evans Street. The funeral was right across the street, and he was buried in the cemetery on Evans Street. We used to go and place dandelions and wildflowers on his grave. He was good as he could be to us kids. Mr. Taney's gravesite was in the middle of other gravesites, and since we were superstitious, we had to say, "Excuse me," or "I'm sorry," each time we stepped over another

Here we are on Easter Sunday. I'm on the right, leaning in.

Me and Rosemary Rodriquez

gravesite to get to Mr. Taney's. After Mr. Taney died, the Rodriguez family moved in around 1973. There were about five girls and one boy, and the Rodriguez girls were all beautiful. I dated Rosemary, Richard White dated Linda, and Duke Coleman later dated Carmen. Cindy and Jacquie were too young. The one Rodriquez boy was Billy.

Joleen and Francine Temperato and Debbie and Lori Carey lived down the street on Andes Ave. Denise and

My family in my younger days. That's me on the bottom left.

Claudine Otti lived on the corner of Evans and Andes for a short time. The Conervalli family of all girls lived on the corner of Andes and Herbert, and another Conervalli family of girls lived on the corner of Middle and Herbert Streets. The youngest girl married Bobby Bero. Bobby was a good lacrosse player, and he was a good athlete like his older brothers Don and Tommy. They lived on Maxwell Avenue. The daughters in both Conervalli families were all beautiful. We lived near the railroad tracks and Route 5 and 20 – Middle and Evans Streets. Me and my brother Barron would easily cross over Route 5 and 20 to go to Seneca Lake to swim. Tom DeJohn lived on Herbert Street, and there was a girl named Barb that lived on the corner of Andes and Herbert.

It was a sad day when Theresa Panetta passed in June 1987. She died in a tragic boating accident on Seneca Lake. She was with a friend and they hit the light pier that used to sit on the lake. I'm glad they removed that damn pier. I was in college in 1975 when I received her wedding invitation. The wedding was at Saint Francis Church, and the reception was at Club 86. She moved into a house across the street from where she grew up on Genesee Street. Theresa was a dear friend, and she was loved by everyone in Geneva. Theresa R.I.P.

Throughout my life, I have had the privilege to watch many great athletes from Geneva and beyond—athletes who made their mark at the high school, college and even professional levels. I want to honor some of the standouts in this chapter.

GENEVA: As a youngster there were many Geneva athletes I looked up to; I wanted to be like them, and I wanted to represent their names when I played. My favorite Geneva athlete growing up was a guy named Chuckie Damic. He was short in size, but he backed a punch. He was a couple of grades ahead of me, and his nickname was "Butkus." I remember one day we were watching the seniors practice and they were hitting the sled. I heard Coach McDonald ask the team to turn the sled around so they could hit it back in the opposite direction. They were all tired. I remember the smallest guy on the team stepped up and hit the sled turning it around alone. I asked some of the other guys, who was that? They said 'Chuckie Damic', that is when I became his biggest fan. Small but he had the biggest heart on

Mark Pitifer and Mark Wilson

the G.H.S. football team. I last saw Chuckie bartending at a bar in Waterloo. My second favorite Geneva athlete was a guy named Eddie Lathey, a football player who seemed to always have dust in the air around him because he played so physically. They both graduated ahead of me probably around 1973.

The first experience I had in watching a true Geneva great was watching a girl named Roxanne Logue, a track star who held the Geneva high school record for a long time. I saw her run at Loman Field around 1964. Roxanne was finally upset by a girl named Cynthia Yawn. Some of my other favorite athletes were Steve Lahr, Ron Patrick, Henry Howard, Leo Dinan, Donnie Williams and Richie Blue.

I believe the best GHS men's basketball team was the 1977 team with Marvin Sapp, Andy Collier, Mark Wilson, and Mark Pitifer. Mark Wilson sadly passed away due to cancer he was like a brother. He and I had a lot of the same issues. I would like to point out that Mary Murphy was probably the best basketball female player for GHS; numbers do not lie, and she has them. Joe Iaconis was a sports announcer when I played. He was on the board of directors for the Geneva Sports Hall of Fame, and he was very informative on any sports question you had for him. Tyrone L. Collins, who graduated from GHS in 2006, is one impressive athlete to come out of Geneva, and Vincent Ray,

1975 Rochester War Memorial. Standing Charles Pinkard, Jim Henderson, my brother Butch Frank, Glen Hudson, Albert Sellers. Kneeling: Nate Burke, Richie Blue, Randy Richmond and Harold Cuda Fryer.

was a Geneva great in basketball; he played college in Hawaii and Sweden. Let me not forget Mr. Carl Wenzel of Geneva, who I have a great deal of respect for. I first saw him play in the Lincoln First tournament at the War Memorial. It was 1974, and I went to that tournament to watch my cousin Ron and Dan Gilliam play for Brockport versus St. John's. My cousin Ron Gillam passed away in 2018 from a heart attack. He was a great player; he led the nation in scoring Brockport State in 1972 season. Wenzel was a sharpshooter for St. John's — he had a funny release, but it was deadly. Later I played in the Geneva city league games against Carl. He played for a team called Truck Town, and they were the team to beat. They had Nick Fererri, Dan Davids, John Fitzgerald, Steve Fitzgerald, and Dave Sweeney. I remember a game when I was guarding Carl, and he said, "Bronson, give me a shot." I said, "Carl, I would let you shoot, but you never miss." Dennis 'Gomer' Riccione and Gary Strait were two other Geneva High basketball greats; they played three years ahead of me.

I cannot forget Geneva's Mary Murphy; she played basketball and baseball and she bowled. I remember a guy Bill Rupert, "Rupe," who was short and stocky and a nice guy. He was a good softball player, and I also played against him in city league basketball in the late '70s. Marc and Guy VanArsdale were also Geneva greats. They both went to Hobart and did extremely well. Marc was an unbelievable attackman. I missed both of their careers when I was in the U.S. Navy from 1981 to 1984. I am in touch with Marc these days. He is now coaching for Loyola University Maryland lacrosse.

One summer league Marc put an excellent move on me that proved he was a great. It was a roll dodge – I'll never forget it. Marc attended Hobart from 1982 to 1985, and he was an assistant coach with Virginia lacrosse for almost fifteen years. Marc was named the coach for the South All-Stars for the prestigious North-South All-Star lacrosse game in 2001. Marc graduated magna cum laude as a history major, and in 1985 he was a first team All-American. He was MVP for two national championship games, in 1983 and 1985 and a four-time national champion. He is what you call 'decorated.' Athletes will tell you numbers don't lie, and Marc VanArsdale has the numbers. Coaching Loyola Md., I went to his game in 2016 when they played UNC. I was able to speak with Mark briefly after that game. During that game I decided to watch Mark to see what type of coach he was. I saw how he spoke and how the players listened and reacted to his speech. I was impressed and said to myself, "He's a good coach." In 2017, when they played Duke, he left tickets for me at the gate. I consider Mark a true friend.

Guy VanArsdale, who graduated in 1984, played goalie for Hobart. He was awarded the nation's top goalie award for three years in a row. I remember one summer league lacrosse game when Guy yelled at me for not playing defense in front of my man. I could never understand why, when the ball is at the other end of the field, a defenseman plays 'in front' of the attackman. I wanted to play behind, as to not let him beat me to the goal. I always stayed close enough to the attackman and the midline so that if the ball went to the midline, I could

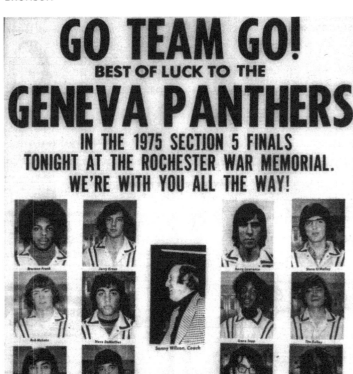

GO TEAM GO!
BEST OF LUCK TO THE
GENEVA PANTHERS
IN THE 1975 SECTION 5 FINALS
TONIGHT AT THE ROCHESTER WAR MEMORIAL.
WE'RE WITH YOU ALL THE WAY!

be there before the ball got there. I was a lot faster than the defenseman Guy was probably used to playing with. I did not explain to Guy why I played behind. I respected him. Plus, he had played with one of my favorite Hobart lax players, Kevin Martin.

I believe Donte Reed was the most talented of all the Geneva athletes. I remember a kid named Steve DeMatties, who is now the owner of a professional baseball organization in Florida. His dad was a respected guy in Ge-

Geneva High School, 1975.
Jimmy Cardinale in the
background

neva – Ju Ju DeMatties. Steve was a very good baseball catcher, and he is now in the Geneva Sports Hall of Fame. He had a great run while playing for Ithaca College. When I was around fifteen, there was a guy named Al Klestinic who was there when my basketball game went into a different gear. He was the first guard that I really focused on watching his body fakes, which helped my defense quite a bit. Allie used to referee the city league basketball games back in the late 1970s. During one game, one of the players spit on Allie for allegedly making a bad call. I and the other blacks were very upset at him. Allie was a well-respected person to us, and he did not deserve to get spit on.

Joe Crisanti was a DeSales guy who was another Geneva great. DeSales also had the great Jody Lavin, who graduated from DeSales in 1978. Jody had great numbers. I wonder if she and Mary Murphy ever met on the court. Joe Crisanti was a great guy, well-respected on and off the court. DeSales also had the notorious Red Millis, who met his match one day at Gulvin's Park. When I coached the DeSales girls team in 1985, it was said that Tom Donahue's daughter was going to be a great player.

DeSales also had one of my favorite athletes, Bootie Gringeri. In life we never know who we will be in contact with years later, and for me to be in contact with Bootie Gringeri is a blessing. While writing this book I contacted Bootie through our LinkedIn accounts. Bootie was a natural athlete, proved by the fact that he walked on to the lacrosse team at Hobart College and played at a high level within a year. I remember him being a handsome Italian guy who was friendly.

Bootie wanted me to mention the DeSales team of 1971. I told Bootie I recall him marrying a really pretty girl whose last name was Pitifer. He told me that her name was Debbie, and she became his wife in 1982. Bootie graduated from DeSales in 1973 where he played basketball and football. Bootie went to Hobart, which was a nationally known lacrosse school. He was self-taught. As a freshman he only played long stick middie, defense and middie. Bootie was a starter as a sophomore, playing the crease on defense. They lost the national championship in 1975 to Cortland, and in 1976 they beat Adelphi to win the national title. Bootie was disappointed that he did not win All-American Honors. (I'm sure he deserved that award).

Bootie and I know a lot of the same athletes. I mentioned a guy I played on the Miller Lacrosse team with named Bo Raleigh, and Bootie said that he knew him because they both attended Hobart and Bo was the Hobart quarterback. I knew Bo because he was a defensive man on the Miller lacrosse team I played for. I also mentioned an awesome defensive man for Hobart named Kevin Martin, who Bootie knew from Cortland. Bootie and I also both knew Ed Howard, who played defense for Hobart. Bootie also mentioned Tom Schardt, which reminded me of a game Schardt played with a patch over his eye. He was still very effective.

SENECA FALLS: When I was young there was a guy named Vinni Giglio from Seneca Falls. I was around fifteen when I first saw him, an Italian guy coming to Gulvin Park to play. He had a California jersey on, and he was good. In later years we became close friends. He had a basketball tournament in Seneca Falls in the late 70s, and we won that tournament. I hear he now lives in California. There was another guy from Seneca Falls named Jeff Farney. He was a heck of a basketball player, and he was also a very good baseball player. Joe Procelli and Gene Geovannini were great shooters from Seneca Falls. Gene played for a short time for Elmira College, which is where he met my brother Barron, who became an All-American there. Tom Sage was also a Seneca Falls great. The entire Verkey family — Rod, Gary and Dennis — were tough players. Seneca Falls had two sisters Sandy and Cheryl, wish I could remember their last name. I last saw them at a bar called Filthy McNasty's around 1976...

Lu Ann Davids

Judy Nicit

ROMULUS: There was a guy named Glen Hudson who was a very good ballplayer. He played overseas for a long time. He once told me how much better I had gotten from the previous summer. That gave me confidence – I appreciated those words from him. Romulus had a legendary coach in Mr. Alvaro. Dan, Leo and Ted Davids were also from Romulus. I worked with them at the American Can Company in Geneva, and I dated their sister Lu Ann in 1974. In 1977 I bought a 1971 Super Bee car from Ted Davids. It was a muscle car. I loved that car. Someday I'd like to buy another. Romulus also had a guy named Dave Thompson who was a good basketball player. Daiman Nicholson was also a tough player, and Barney Farnsworth was a good rebounder.

MARCUS WHITMAN: In 1971 I went to a GHS basketball game and saw what looked like a giant. His name was Chris Iverson. He was at least 6-foot-7 and I never saw a man that tall. He is now the owner of Iverson construction, which is his own major construction company in Penn Yan. I also need to mention Steve Bodine and Dan Harris.

A stickup and an escape

Ted Williams (14) of Geneva looks like a bandit who has just stuck up three Newark Reds and now is making his escape as he goes after a loose ball during action last night. Newark victims of the holdup were Bob Bushart (42), Mike Tanea (24) and Chip Bloomer (52). (Times photo).

WATERLOO: Pat Dunlea was deadly, a sharpshooter. They also had a female great in Kim Sucliffe, and another talented player named John Schweitz, who was probably the best basketball player to come out of the Finger Lakes. He stood 6-foot-5 and went to college in Richmond, Va. He played for an NBA practice team out west. He had an older brother, Steve, who set records at Hartwick College. Steve passed away way too young — he was a good guy. I remember John asking me to play summer league with him and his brother in Cortland, N.Y. One thing

Coach Gary Miller, George Rivers and Mike Tanea. George was the fastest player I ever played against and Mike was a Newark great.

always stuck out for me about Steve, whenever I went to his Cortland home before games to get ready. He would always be holding his son Kyle in one hand and a beach ball in the same hand while tying his sneakers. He did that with ease. NFL coach Tom Coughlin, who led the New York Giants and the Jacksonville Jaguars,

Mike Kennedy, a very close friend from Canandaigua

also comes from Waterloo. Another great from Waterloo was Mark Dunn.

NEWARK: Newark had some basketball greats as well. In 1973 I remember my brother Barron jumping center tip, standing six feet tall against Chip Blummer, who was all of 6-feet-5 from Newark. In 1973–'74 Jeff Peters and Bob Bushart played for Newark; Bushart was my favorite. Newark also had Jim-

The team from Kendall High School. The tall guy is Roosevelt Bouie, who went on to play for Syracuse University. He's an all-time shot blocker and a good friend.

my and George Rivers. They were greats. We won several basketball tournaments at the Alex Eligh Gym in Newark. My parole officer Ms. Sheila Tanea was from Newark. She was my parole officer for five years, and she gave me no leeway. She once said there is a big debate on who was the best basketball player between Tim and Mike Tanea. I along with many others would say Mike. Mike could make his own moves and get a shot. Tim needed a pick to get free. Plus, Tim's release on his shot was a lot lower than Mike's. However, Tim was a Newark great as well. I last saw Tim when I was coaching the DeSales girls around 1985. He was coaching a youth team from Newark.

CANANDAIGUA: Mike Kennedy, a left-handed point guard and a good friend of mine, played point guard for Canandaigua. We are still friends to this day and are in constant contact. EVERYONE in Canandaigua knows Mike. We first became friends in 1974 our junior year. When I got arrested he went to the Judge and pleaded for me. He stayed in touch with me throughout my incarceration. I came home and lived in Canandaigua he helped me to get back on my feet. Whenever I'm home I stop by his house and say hello. We talk on the phone on occasions. He always reminds me of a time when I was on an all star basketball team that played against a Russian team. Everyone in Canandaigua knows Mike. He worked for Pactiv over 20 years and his dad was once the mayor of Canandaigua. I dated Missi Himes for several years. She always told me how her parents liked me. She had a friend named Patty Sheraton who had long beautiful hair back then, and Patty now works for Martin Muehe, one of the best attorneys in Canandaigua. Patty recently told me that Jeff Johnson passed away. He operated a funeral home in Canandaigua. Everyone in Canandaigua partied at Jeff Johnson's cottage, including myself several times. Canandaigua has family with the last name Lacrosse. I played lacrosse against one of the boys and when I worked at the Canandaigua Veterans Administration. The father was brought in, he was a very nice man, we talked sports alot.

Canandaigua also has Mr. Dan Wegman, the founder of the Wegman's grocery chain. I have been attempting to speak with him for years. I have written him several letters requesting an interview, job and to help promote his annual three-on-three basketball tournament. I've heard people praise his dad, who began that dynasty. Maybe one day I'll finally get to meet him. Danny recently opened several Wegman's store's here in the Raleigh, NC area. There's a nice lady named Renee who works for Dan Wegman. There was

Wegmans store in Raleigh NC

another guy, Bill Scharr, who went on to play quarterback for Syracuse University. He was also very good in lacrosse. Fred White, John Greene, Tom Pelton and Wayne Marks were great players for Canandaigua.

MIDLAKES: Mikki DePorter was a good basketball player from Midlakes, as well as a coach named Pete Herman who later went on to coach the US Navy Basketball Team. Mikki's brothers were Tom and Al DePorter. I also knew Patsy Schroeder and Al Porter. I was close friends with Julie Philiips, she took me to her home and I met her mom. There was also a girl that had pictures of me inside of her locker, Kristen Bidleman. Midlakes also had Anthony and Allen Hudson, who are true friends. Anthony now lives in California and has every degree you can imagine, and Allen lives in Ohio. I remember Allen being a very good point guard. One day we were playing basketball at Gulvin Park, Allen was playing with a cast on his wrist and he was still very effective. It was unbelievable. Both nice guys and close friends.

SOUTH SENECA: I played against Scott McDonald in the city basketball league. He was a physical banger in the paint like I was. I enjoyed playing against him, because he made me a better player. I believe he had a bad back or leg. He limped up and down the court, but he was a force to reckon with. Steve McShain was also good.

LYONS: Jo Jo Jackson graduated from Lyons Central High around 1974. They had a good team that barely beat Geneva in 1974. They also had Dan Thomas and Chris (Omar) Williams. Longtime Syracuse head basketball coach Jim Boeheim is also from Lyons.

PENN YAN: Penn Yan, of course, had the Collins family. Tony made it to the NFL. He dated my sister Brenda, and I would take her down to East Carolina University in the 1977-1979 and watch him play. Morris Collins was probably the best high school football player in Penn Yan history. Penn Yan had a dear friend of mine, Austin Narewski, who died way too young in June 2010 due to a motorcycle accident. My dear friend Sandra Snyder is his grandma. I have his name tattooed on my rib cage, along with the names of twelve others. Going to Penn Yan was dangerous for a black person back in the day. If we ever went there, we made sure we had at least five of us blacks, thinking there was safety in numbers.

HOBART: I played a lot of sports with and against some Hobart greats. The first that comes to mind is a football great named Don Aleksiewicz – we all called him A.Z. He once took me on a motorcycle ride and

Hobart and William Smith Colleges

Colleges mourn Hall of Famer Ed Howard
Ken DeBolt
Statesmen Athletic Association
Posted: 6/18/2012 4:02:00 PM
The Hobart and William Smith Colleges' community is mourning the loss of Hobart Athletics Hall of Famer Edward I. Howard '79. The two-time lacrosse All-American died unexpectedly on Saturday, June 16.

Visitation is scheduled for 6-8 p.m. on Thursday, June 21 at Kimble Funeral Home, 1 Hamilton Ave., Princeton, N.J. A private, family service will be held later.

Howard came to Hobart as a basketball recruit from Canisius High School in Buffalo, N.Y. He traded the basketball for a lacrosse stick and the rest is one of the truly remarkable stories in Hobart's rich lacrosse history. Howard was a four-year letterman on defense in lacrosse, helping the Statesmen win NCAA Division II National Championships in 1976 and 1977. Hobart posted an impressive 49-8 record during his four seasons on campus, including a perfect 15-0 mark in 1977. As a senior, Howard served as team co-captain, played in the North-South All-Star Game, and earned the Babe Kraus Memorial Award as the Hobart College Athlete of the Year.

A history major, Howard built his career in the insurance industry, most recently serving as a vice president for Chubb & Son.

Howard recently joined the Statesmen Athletic Association Board of Directors and was inducted into the Hobart College Athletic Hall of Fame in 2003.

"His teammates, coaches and friends will tell you that Ed Howard, in every walk of his life, was a superb Statesman," Hobart Athletics Director Mike Hanna says.

– never again. He was aggressive in everything he did. Great Guy. Bootie said he sadly passed away a few years ago. A black player Ed Howard, another self-taught Hobart defensive great, passed away about five years ago also. Bootie asked me to Google Don Aleksiewicz, so I did and wrote a small quote on his obituary on Legacy. com. I wrote about how I would go to the Hobart football games in 1971 and watch him run over opponents. We would climb the fence and watch him play until our hands got numb, then wait for the offense to take the field again before climbing the fence again to watch him. I finally met him around 1977, when he played in some of our Geneva summer league lacrosse games.

The next Hobart great was a guy named Terry Corcoran, who graduated from Hobart in 1978. He was a big redheaded attackman from East Corning. He was at least 6-foot-5 and solid. I first remember seeing pictures of him on the wall at a bar on Hobart Campus called Twin Oaks. He had a brother named Joe who also played defense for Hobart. I first met Terry around 1977 while playing for the Miller Lacrosse Team out of Syracuse. I followed Terry's career when he coached Washington College, Skidmore, Wabash and University of Massachusetts Dartmouth. I consider Terry a true friend. My favorite Hobart lax player was a guy name Mark Darcangelo. He was from Corning East, a powerhouse school. He used to toy with me during summer league lacrosse games and practices. He was teaching me, and I was learning from one of the best. I would see him teaching summer camps at Hobart. He also had an older brother that played for the USA team.

In September 2018 Mr. Dave Urick was honored with having the Bowell Field also named the Mr. Dave J. Urick field. He deserved it; he was a great guy. On the 1980 Hobart lacrosse team there was a guy named Jon Feinstein from Long Island. He would always tell me how smooth I threw the ball. He passed away at the age of 27, which is very sad. I read that he did things for underprivileged children all over, including the Geneva area, sending inner-city kids to Hobart lacrosse camp and starting the first Harlem Middle School lacrosse team. Jon, thank you for always being nice to me and may you rest in peace. Google the Jon Feinstein Memorial Fund.

Kevin Martin from Cortland was unbelievable on defense. Ed Howard was a black player who was a walk-on and received two All-America honors. He sadly passed away 2012. He was a true friend. Mac Nelson was another black walk-on lacrosse player, and Rick Blick was a great goalie for Hobart.

BRONSON

Geneva and its beautiful females

Geneva had its share of beautiful females. Lisa Alexander, Pam O'Neil, Edeen and Jeanie Lisi, Anita DePaula, Jacquie Taras, Dale Easton, Lu An Gillotti, Jill Harding, Cindy Barrody, Robin and Sue Fegley, Rosemary Rodriguez, Cindy Santiago and Machelle Richmond. Just to name a few. However, I cannot leave out Lisa George who I literally saw stop traffic.

Pam O'Neil was the most perfect blonde-haired blue-eyed beauty that you would ever see. The most beautiful girl I dated was Rosemary Rodriguez in 1973. She was a picture-perfect Latina. Rosemary had sisters named Carmen, Linda, Geishia, Jackie and Cindy, and they were all beautiful.

The great DeSales High School girls basketball team in the 1984-'85 season was coached by myself, Steve Muzzi and Frank Payne. That team was a coach's dream.

1984-'85 DeSales High School girls basketball team

The starting five was Lisa Cote, Babette and Stephanie DeVaney, Chrissy Guinan and Alesha Priebe. Coming off the bench the team had Sue Maher, Marci MacLaren,

Rosemary Rodriguez

Christine Cosentino, Kirsten Sindoni and Machelle Trotta. That team was loaded with talent. Lisa was a dominator in the paint. I showed her a how to post her player up and I taught her the drop-step move. She mastered it. Alesha Priebe improved so much each practice and game, especially her ball handling skills. She never turned the ball over. I taught her how to split two defenders, and I also showed her how to push the ball instead of just dribbling it. Lisa Cote's mom's name was Annette and she and Lisa's grandma were very nice to me. They lived on Kirkwood avenue. My mom would tell me that Annette would have Lisa come over and speak to my mom at the Bingo hall. Lisa's

Lisa Cote

mom would always come over and speak with me after the games. I believe Annette now lives in Florida.

Babette was the heart and soul of that team. She was stronger than most of the guards she played against. She was fearless, the best I've coached. Her sister Stephanie was also a dominator in the paint, a strong rebounder on both ends of the court. She reminded me of the way I played. She got the ball and drove hard to the basket. Both DeVaneys were fearless. Chrissy Guinan was probably the best all-around player on the team. She just needed to be motivated to play harder; I guess she was shy on the court. But once I got her going, her numbers shot up — her scoring and her defense. In a high school playoff game Chrissy sprained her ankle really bad. She sat there and could not get up. Her dad walked with a cane. He came out of the stands, walked down to the court, put his cane over his arm, picked Chrissy up and carried her back to the bench. She had a good career at

Nazareth College. Maureen Quigley was tall. She worked well in paint with Lisa. Maureen got a lot of rebounds on the weak side, which was a big plus. Her mom and dad were also tall also, so I saw where she got her height.

Kirsten Sindoni was a battler. She had the biggest heart on the team. When I would scrimmage with the team, I can remember Kirsten pushing and shoving me. I also coached Kirsten in 1977 at St. Francis School. Michelle Trotta came in off the bench and did well. She played defense very well. She liked trapping. Christine Cosentino was a sharpshooter. She hustled, and she loved shooting from the corner. Last was Sue Maher. She did

Stacey Marstiener

not play her junior year due to injury. She played her senior year, and she proved everything I had heard of her. Kirsten would always brag about, "Just wait 'til Sue comes back next season." That next season came, and I understood what Kirsten meant. Sue was a great shooter. I remember an underclassman named Stacey Marstiener. She was tall and was going to be a great player. Her mom was also tall. That 1984-'85 team made it as far as winning the Section 5 class D all-tournament team. They (we) also won the NYSPHSAA Far West regionals, and we made it to the semifinals of States. That team went that far without hav-ing one designed play on offense, and on defense they played zone. We never pressed on defense. I tried to get the coach to include a designed play for Lisa, but he did not know how. I also wanted him to press on defense, because that team had so many great athletes. I just wish they would have had at least one designed play not only for Lisa, but for Chrissy, Sue and Babette. Babette could have taken on any guard she faced.

Claudine Rinaldo

Mary Rinaldo

I coached Lisa, Kirsten and Chrissy back in 1978, when they played for Saint Frances. Mary and Claudine Rinaldo played for the 1978 Saint Frances team also, and their parents James and Carol Rinaldo were like family to me. If that team would have had one set play for each player they would have won States easily, or Regionals.

Picture of Team

In 1986 I began working for New York State Electric & Gas Company in Lockport, N.Y. I contacted one of the two high schools there to request a coaching position. One of their schools was named DeSales High school, the same name as the Geneva team. It was also a small Catholic school. The coach, Lisa accepted me as her assistant. That team had average players—not as good as my other DeSales team in Geneva, but they competed. That team had some very good designed plays.

I believe the most respected person in Geneva History was Mr. Guy Spader. There should not only be a statue of him outside of G.H.S.; there should be a statue of him in Geneva – period. I first laid eyes on this great man in 1968, when I was eleven years old. My older brother Butch took me to my first basketball game, at the now-North Street Elementary School. I remember walking in that gym, and the smell of the cigarettes was foreign to me. At that time you were allowed to smoke cigarettes in a gymnasium. My eyes started to burn, and I got sick. I went into the men's locker room and threw up. Instead of me watching the basketball game, I found myself watching the coach and imagining myself as one of the players, with him coaching me. I wondered if when I got big I would one day play for him. As he subbed the players in and out of the game, I imagined it was me.

By the time I got to high school Mr. Spader had taken the athletic director position. I got to know him around 1972. I now think of the many gray hairs I gave him during my high school years, and I'm not proud of any of them. I was an athlete who pushed the boundaries, and Mr. Spader was an athletic director who did not play that game. He was a very kind man, and he stood his ground. He had a stare that would cut right through you. As time went on I remember not holding any eye contact with him, because I knew what he was saying to me and it was not nice. As a junior in 1974 I wore a big afro, and at times I had it braided. Mr. Spader did not like braided hair and he often let me know it. He would tell me it looked like a horse's ass. What he disliked most was when I wore my hair braided during basketball games. Ouch… I would have to stay away from him for a few days after that. I say that Mr. Spader is the most respected, because he was respected by most people that I knew throughout Geneva.

I remember when I was around twelve years old, watching the older guys playing horse and imagining one day I was going to be big like them. Suddenly they stopped playing and began to straighten out their clothing, focusing on behaving themselves. Their focus went to some man who had just walked up. I looked at the man and back at the older guys and I remember him as being the same man I saw coaching that basketball team that night — Mr. Spader. I also recall being at another event around the same age and I watching the older guys, thinking that one day I would be big too. As I watched these big boys, I noticed they were all seemed to be standing at attention, and they all had on these fancy jackets with the sleeves made of leather. I later realized they were the Varsity Club. I continued to look at them and noticed that man again — Mr. Spader. I said to myself, *That man must be important.* As the years went on, probably around 1974, we were outside at an event and there was a guy there named Richard Fowler who was the most notorious, feared person in Geneva history. Richard was a graduate of GHS, and he was feared by most. I noticed Richard and Mr. Spader were there and they were walking and were about to cross each other's path. I said to myself, *Here we go.* I wanted to see who blinked first or who spoke first between these two giants. I knew neither person gave an inch to anybody. This would tell it all. I watched Richard; he had not seen Mr. Spader coming yet. Richard finally looked up and saw Mr. Spader coming, and then he hesitated, straightened his clothing and spoke first to Mr. Spader. That is when I knew who the most respected person in Geneva was.

In approximately 1977 I had a basketball travel team with myself, my brother Barron, Gene and Marvin Sapp and Randy Hudson. We traveled throughout the Finger Lakes playing in and winning a lot of unlimited basketball tournaments. There was a tournament in Elmira at Southside High School, and we needed jerseys to play. Since it was my team, the guys suggested that I contact Mr. Spader and ask him for some of the old GHS basketball jerseys. I was afraid, thinking of the hard time I gave Mr. Spader in high school. Now I have the nerve to ask him for jerseys? It took me two days to get up the nerve to call him. I asked for the jerseys, explained the tournament, and mentioned the other guys' names. Just in case he cursed me out, I figured they would get it too. Before I finished asking him, he said, "Come and get them." I remember feeling happiness and sadness. Here's a man who I thought did not like me because I gave him gray hairs in high school, and now he was telling me to come and get jerseys. Before I hung up the phone, I remember feeling shame

Guy Spader

and embarrassment, thinking of the hard times I had given this man.

He told me to come to his office the following morning to pick up the jerseys at 10 'o'clock. There was no way I was going to be late for that appointment. I remember getting to the GHS parking lot at 9:30 a.m. I sat there watching the clock tick down to one minute before 10 a.m. and went in. I walked in, and he had fifteen GHS jerseys sitting on the table for me. He said all he asked was that I brought them back the same way I took them. I said OK and thanked him. We won that basketball tournament at Southside High School. I remember ironing those jerseys twice, and went to Madia's store to get some spray starch to iron those jerseys before returning them. Mr. Spader passed away in 2016. I did not find out until approximately a week after he passed, from my brother Barron. Mr. Spader was a true great. I was upset with my brother for telling me late. There should be a statue of Mr. Spader in Geneva, or at least at Geneva High.

The Way Forward

July 2014 was bittersweet for me. I had just buried my little brother Brian. He was 52, and he passed away from a drug overdose. He passed at the Finger Lakes Inn Hotel on 5 & 20 in Canandaigua. Two weeks later I moved to Garner/Raleigh, North Carolina. I began working for my friend Sandy's son-in-law John Levenbruck, the manager for Interstate Battery Company in Garner. I love the South. The cost of living is low, the weather is great and the people are easygoing. I finally found a two-bedroom country style duplex for $550 a month, which was a steal. I moved in along with my White Pigeons. I quickly noticed how many females there were compared to men. It's at least 20-to-1 female-to-male. I noticed black and white couples, but a white man with a black girl was way different. Since being in the South I've also noticed how beautiful the black women are. I was told

Afterglow

I'd like the memory of me to be a happy one.
I'd like to leave an afterglow of smiles when
life is done. I'd like to leave an echo
whispering softly down the ways, of happy
times and laughing times and bright and sunny
days. I'd like the tears of those who grieve, to
dry before the sun; of happy memories that I
leave when life is done.

Homegoing Celebration

in honor of

Brian David Frank Sr.

June 13, 1961 – April 11, 2014

Mt. Olive Missionary Baptist Church
70 Clark Street.
Geneva, New York
Rev. Donald Golden

Pall Bearers:

Jeffrey Bostic Jr.	Marvin Sapp
James Brandenburg	Bill English
Philip Brandenburg Jr.	Jeff Mallard

April 16, 2014
Viewing 10am
Service 11am
Burial to Follow at Glenwood Cemetery

the further you go South the more beautiful the black women get. It's true. Being from the North I have dated many white girls. Since I moved down here I have been approached by white girls, but I cannot see myself with a white girl in the south. It's a different feel and look.

In October 2014 I began working for the Durham Veterans Administration, but I was released from the VA due to reporting my supervisor for telling fellow employees about my past. I reported him on a Tuesday and got released that Friday. In July 2015 I began working for PC construction. I had never worked with Hispanics who were undocumented, and I never realized how racist they were. Illegals do not like black men, but they love back women. I was called nigger and slave, and my truck was keyed twice. So how so I feel about DACA? (Send 'em home!) The majority of them do not like white or black Americans. I hurt my knee while working for PC Construction and went out on Workman's Compensation. I received $15,000 and resigned. In February 2017 I began working at the Fayetteville Veterans Administration. I loved working at the VA. The hospitality there and the opportunity to serve the veterans is rewarding. I was hired as a temporary worker in food service department and after eight months I was released, which hurt. They call Fayetteville FayettNam, short for Vietnam. But it's not that bad. I've always said, "Stay out of the bad areas and away from bad people you won't have problems."

When I got released from prison, I started keeping white pigeons in my backyard and renting them out for all types of ceremonies, mostly weddings and funerals. I brought my birds with me when I moved to North Carolina; however, I am not receiving much business due to the COVID. I was told that I needed to be on social media. So I finally started a website – ceremonialwhitebirds.com. One problem I was facing with the birds was that the hawks in the South are more aggressive than the hawks in the North, not to mention

Bronson with bird

Ceremonial white birds

during the hot months, June and July, the black snakes come out and they were getting into my bird shed and eating the eggs and baby birds. I have killed several.

People have asked me, what was the hardest part of coming home after doing twenty years? I have said, not hearing from my old friends Marvin and Gene Sapp. I was close to them before I went away. I thought that when I came home I would spend time with them again. That was not the case. I did not hear from them, it hurt. It took me one-and-a-half years before I realized I wasn't going to be spending as much time with them. I had to realize twenty years is a long time, people change, things change. I realized they were now married and had a family. I finally accepted it and moved on. I still miss being with them and call them whenever I'm back in Geneva.

The second hardest thing was speaking to a female. After all those years I was used to talking to men, not ladies. When talking to a female, I would stutter and get nervous.

Top Row: Gene Sapp, Myself, Tim Northrup, Piper VanAlstyne, Anthony Woody. Bottom Row: Brian Frank and Marvin Sapp.

Looking into the eyes of a female who had makeup on and smelled nice was entirely different from what I was used to. I was finally released from parole supervision on March 27, 2014. I remember feeling that the 20-plus years of my nightmare was finally over. I remember buying some beer and placed it in the fridge, but I was so afraid to touch it that it sat there for approximately three weeks before I finally had the nerve to try one.

When I was about 15, around 1972, I began stealing eight-track tape players out of cars. Me and my friend Homer McCoy would look for cars that were unlocked, open the door and kick the eight-track players out. We would sell them for $20. I guess I could blame some of it on not having a dad at home. I now realize that coming up in a single-family home is far different from having both parents. (My dad passed away on August 30, 1969) He was born in Dresden, N.Y., and he worked for Bouley Construction Co. of Auburn, N.Y. as a mason foreman. He was a member of Trinity Church and member of Bricklayers, Masons and Plasters International Union Local 43, he was also a member of Winnek Post American Legion, having served in World War II. I moved on to hanging around guys who would go to the local college and steal during Spring Break. It's the best time because all of the students were gone, allegedly. I began breaking in at the local college around 1973, and it became a bad habit. I don't remember missing a year of burglarizing up until 1988. Burglaries were my drug of choice. I started burglaries with the other guys, but then I began going on my own. I felt I did not need anyone, and I could get away faster on my own if needed. Most Christmases I would come home with a stereo, speakers, and other items.

As the years went on, I would enter dwellings without taking anything. I was now only there for the adrenaline rush, the high. I would break in and sit until the adrenaline rush went away then I would leave. I can remember going downtown to a club (LTD) and getting the urge to burglarize. I had a jump suit and shoes I would wear, stashed in my car. I would put that on, go burglarize and come back to the club, without stealing anything; that was my high. I needed that adrenaline rush. My burglarizing went from 1973 to 1988. Lord knows I am thankful it's over. When I came home from prison, I would drive past the houses that I had burglarized and feel shame, embarrassment and guilt. I visualized myself going into those windows and felt ashamed. Still do.

BRONSON

Tragedy

In the summer of 1973 we were all swimming at Seneca Lake, pushing each other into the water behind the now chamber of commerce. My friend Larry Bramlett pushed my friend Tat into the water, and I came behind Larry and pushed him in. He went in and did not come up. He was a clown, so we all thought he was playing around as usual. He finally surfaced — his neck was broken. I was the first to reach him; he said he was yelling for me. When I pulled his head above the water, I felt the bone bulging in the back of his neck. I quickly got him out of the water into my car and took him to the Geneva General hospital. They quickly transferred him to the Upstate Hospital in Syracuse. I followed the ambulance and stayed with a friend, Dwight Harrison. He lived in the Wilson Park Projects which was five minutes from the hospital. I was there when they brought him out of the emergency room. He asked me, "What happened? Why can't I move?" I told him he hit a funny bone in his neck and it would take time before his feeling came back. He asked me why did they drill in his head? I did not have an answer. I went to see him every day, and we talked about boxing. He had friends that did not like me and wanted him to not like me either, but he said we would remain friends which meant a lot to me. Larry was the top boxer in Geneva; he had a very bright career. I messed it up. I can remember that day before I left the house I told my mom that I had a feeling something bad was going to happen that day. She said, "Don't say that." I went to the lake, and that is when it happened.

After the third day I was with Larry and some Geneva people came — Bertha Jenkins and Mr. Jenkins and their family. I left and went back to the place where I was staying, which was a five-minute walk. I walked into the house and my friend Dwight said I had a phone call from my Mom. I took the phone and Mom said, "Larry passed away." I told mom that I had just left him five minutes ago. She said it again: "Bronson, he passed." My heart sank. She said my sister Beth was on her way over to pick me up, to bring me home. I came home to tensions between my friends and Larry's so-called friends. They were saying that I did it on purpose, and Larry's younger brother was saying that when he grew up he was going to shoot me.

There was talk that Larry's family from Mississippi was coming to kill me. At the funeral I sat with my friends, and there was tension. I was hurt that I was not chosen as a pall bearer. After the church service I went to help them carry the casket. One of the guys Gerald Nelson said that they were going to carry him and not me. I said No!, Larry was my friend too and I was going to help. We went to the cemetery for the burial.

Afterwards everybody was going to Larry's house to eat. Larry had told me not to worry about them being jerks towards me and my friends. That was the good thing about Larry — everybody liked Larry and he liked everybody. We got to the house and Larry's so-called friends were waiting outside the house.

Larry

We walked past them and went inside, and I sat down. After a minute I saw a lady coming towards me with a plate of food in her hands. She sat beside me and said that she had heard I was a good kid and I came from a good family. She said not to worry about people saying Larry's family was coming from Mississippi to hurt me.

I guessed she was Larry's mom. She handed me the plate of food and assured me there were no hard feelings and she knew I did not hurt Larry on purpose. Being a true Christian, she said Jesus called her son home. To this day whenever I am home in Geneva I make sure I go to her home Ms. Robinson and spend time with her. I also take flowers to his burial site. My dad is buried on the same hill as him. Whenever I see Larry's brother Parnell, I feel so sad. I always apologize to him for what happened in 1973, and he always says he forgives me and knows it was not on purpose. He tells me that I need to forgive myself, which is very difficult for me.

I graduated from Geneva High School in 1975. On graduation night two girls that I was seeing, Shelly Mattice and Sherry Hynick, were arguing. They were both very aggressive. I had been drinking and allowed Sherry to drive my mom's VW. Shelly was upset and let it be. I was still seeing them both. I attended Fulton Montgomery Community College in Johnstown, N.Y. and played basketball there. It was a small college that my brother Barron attended before me. It was known for its basketball team. They were a ranked junior college in New York State. I was nervous going there, but I liked the atmosphere of college life. I became friends with the basketball players. Most of them were from NYC. I started at the point guard position, which was a big difference from playing the forward position in high school. My mom allowed me to take her VW, and it was the most reliable car I had ever had. It started in the bitter cold and got through the highest snow drifts I had ever seen.

During my first year I was approached by a very pretty white girl named Jennifer Quick; she was a blonde-haired blue-eyed beauty. We dated throughout my year there. There were about four black girls at the school, so there were not a lot of black girls to choose from. One night I was out with Jennifer and a black girl approached me, saying that I should be ashamed of myself dating a white girl with a jacket on that had 'Soul' on the back of it. Jennifer was afraid and I thought about cursing the black girl out but decided against it. We just walked away. It was not the first time a black sister either gave me a dirty look or said something to me about dating a white girl. To be honest, coming from Geneva the majority of the girls I had dated were white. However, I dated black and Hispanic girls also. Jennifer came from a very small town called Northville, N.Y. She took me to her home to meet her mom. She once showed up at one of my games with her parents, which made me nervous.

I began smoking weed in college. I had a friend, Gary, who kept urging me to try it, and one day I tried it just to keep him from continuing to ask me. I did not get high the first several times I tried it. But the third time I got high.

FMCC basketball team

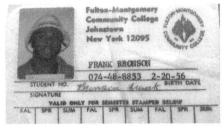

FMCC college ID

Aside from classes, I taught swimming for the youth in Johnstown. The college had a pool, and the kids from the town would come to learn how to swim. I had experience because I had taught swimming the year before at the 4-H camp in Canandaigua during the summer of 1974. That is where I met the great Don and Dottie Ennis from Marcus Whitman. They had a son named Jay. Don Ennis was a great person. He was an athletic man and was well-respected in the Penn Yan area. I honestly did not accomplish much in college. I blew the $2,000 college loan I had and rarely went to class. At the end of the basketball season I quit, which was a bad mistake.

The next year, 1976, I came home and attended Monroe Community College. Again I did not accomplish anything. I came home in 1977, back to Mom. She stayed on me about getting a job. I finally got a very good job working at the American Can Company in Geneva. I was hired at $13 an hour, and that was very good money. I was living at home with my mom for a bit, and small three-bedroom house on Evans and Middle was crowded with myself, Barron, Brenda and Brian. I eventually moved up to my sister and brother-in-law Barbara and David Williams home on Elmwood Place. It was a big house and I moved into the attic, which was huge. I bought a car that was later wrecked by my niece

Jennifer Quick

Kim who had just gotten her permit and thought she knew how to drive. She took it and sideswiped another car. It was repossessed. I then bought a 1971 Super Bee car from a guy from Romulus named Ted Davids. It was a hot rod car and I loved it. When I went into the U.S. Navy in 1981, I left it to my brother Barron and he never took care of it. I was hurt.

BRONSON

U.S. Navy 1981-1984

American Can was laying off around 1980. My time was coming up to be laid off, so I decided to join the Navy. Since American Can was mostly a machine shop, it was brought to my attention that I should go into the service and continue being a part of a machine shop. I went into the Navy in January of 1981 as a machinist repairman. I went to Great Lakes for basic training, and it was freezing there. I was chosen to be a part of a special unit called "Triple Threat" We were a hand-hosen group to perform at all the special events at the base, and I was on the marching team color guard. To this day I miss marching. We had guys who sang, a flag team, and a drum team. We were able to cut the lunch line, and the other teams did not like it. After ten weeks of basic training. I was sent to my "A-School," machinist repairman school in San Diego. The moment we got off the plane we noticed the difference in

Me in my Navy uniform

the temperature and one of the guys commented on how beautiful California girls are. He was right; they were beautiful. I noticed how many Asian people from the Philippines were there, also.

I attended machinist repairman school for eight weeks and then returned home to Geneva for two weeks before reporting to my ship – USS Guadalcanal. The USS Guadalcanal was at sea, on deployment already in Italy, so I had to catch a 747 to Spain. I stayed in Spain for two weeks before finally reporting to the ship in Italy, and I was in awe when I saw that HUGE ship.

It was an LPH-7, which stood for Landing Platform Helicopter Ship. It held approximately 500 Navy guys and 1,500 Marines. It was designed to carry the Marines to their destination, and from there they would fly off the ship using the 40-plus different type of helicopters that were on board. I reported to the engineering department and was taken below deck to my bunk. I heard an announcement for anyone wanting to play on the ship's basketball team. I went to the quarterdeck, and they asked who I was since I had just arrived. I introduced myself and became a part of the basketball team, which included guys from all over. We had a pretty good team. The machine shop was below deck, located between the engine room and the boiler room. So, it was not only HOT but very NOISY. There were times when I was working on the lathe or mill machine and the ship would be rolling sideways and up and down. I had to take off .001 an inch off a part while trying to keep my balance. But for the most part we never felt much of a wave because of the size of the ship; it was huge. I remember getting lost when I first came aboard ship.

In the Navy I saw sights, horizons and sunsets that were awesome. Most of the time all we saw was water and sky. The first port I visited was Naples, Italy. It was dirty and that was the first time that I saw slums. Italy is not what the pictures show. There were pools of urine and shit floating down the streets and clothes hanging out of the windows to dry. It was not what I thought it would be. The people drive fast in these small cars and there are motor bikes all over. Naples had some nice clothes. I bought a pair of shoes and shorts. That was the first time I was there, I would return several more times throughout my Navy years. I remember going to an island off the coast called Capri. It was a tourist island. My friend Kim Khoury said she was there years later for schooling. I was surprised at how much bigger the fruit was on Capri — the lemons and grapes were huge. I remember going through the strait between Italy and Sicily. It was beautiful. Seeing houses on both sides of the mountains was an unbelievable sight. We headed north to Norway and Sweden, and the sight of the mountains was breathtaking. We ported in Norway. There was not much for us to do there – we were very bored. We also visited Denmark and Sweden.

We left Scandinavia after a few weeks and headed back down to Spain. We docked in Mojacar, Spain; some people called it Rota. It was a small city, with nice people, and it had one nightclub. There wasn't much happening there either. From there we went to a small island called Palma in Spain, and I met a very pretty Spanish girl name Paola. She took me home and I stayed with her the entire two weeks we were there. She treated me like a king. She had a friend named Gloria who spoke English. Paola did not, but we managed. I would say something in English and she would always say, "No problemo."

From there we headed back to the States. It took us two weeks to get back to Norfolk, Virginia. We did military exercises with other ships and the Marines on the way back home. I remember us stopping in the middle of the ocean to go swimming. There was no way I was jumping into that ocean. There were small boats in the water to protect the swimmers from sharks, just

USS Guadalcanal

in case, but I was not taking the chance. We played basketball on the top deck, and some guys were playing Frisbee. When the ball or Frisbee went overboard, that was it. It was gone.

After being out for six months, we settled in when we got back to Norfolk. Sleeping on the ship was cool; it was like sleeping on a waterbed. Hearing and feeling the waves was nice. That New Year's Eve I went to a club and met my military girlfriend, Sharon Hembry. She was a very beautiful black girl from Hampton, Va. She was with some guy, but she left him and wanted me. We went outside to sit in her car, but he came out and was kicking the bumper of the car. She got out and told him to stop because she was with me. He left. I dated

Sharon the entire time I stationed in Norfolk, from 1981 to 1984. After Sharon, I dated Katrina Nikki Graham. We are still friends to this day.

I was close friends with a guy named Harold who was from Tuskegee, Alabama. He was married and had two children, they had an apartment off base and I would go over to his place with his family. He was an E-4 machinist mate. He showed me Virginia Beach, but I was

Sharon Hembry

not impressed. We were home for several months and then the USS Guadalcanal pulled out again. After two weeks of travel, our first stop was usually Mojacar, Spain, and after that it was usually Naples, Italy. The Italians would always be out trying to sell items. They called us all Joe. They would say, "Hey Joe, you wanted to buy…?" I remember the scooters and small sports cars, which they drove really fast through the streets. There was not much to do there. Not even the prostitutes looked attractive. It was dirty. Leaving there, we went to Monaco, France.

Katrina Nikki Graham with her kitty, Aziza, and me

It was very nice and the beaches were topless. It seemed to be for the rich, but they had their share of poor areas also. We were there for about a week and then went to Genoa, Italy. It was a military port, so we got a lot of food. I helped stock the freezer. The Navy had the best food you could imagine. If you can imagine it, I was actually tired of steak and lobster. The lobsters were big and very good. We then went down the coast again through the strait of Italy and Sicily. I always made sure I was out on the deck when we went through that strait – it was so beautiful on both sides.

We went up the coast to Venice, which was another tourist city. It was water, water, water. Everyone got around on boats or those gondolas. It seemed to be a rich city, but I am sure if I had gone further into the city I would have seen something different. They never show you the bad parts of these cities. I was not impressed. I was glad to leave. We left there and went down the coast towards Africa. We were supposed to go to Mombasa, Africa, but something was wrong with one of the boilers and we did not have the power to go up and down the Red Sea through the Gulf of Suez. So we went and sat off the Island of Crete.

We soon returned to Norfolk. Virginia may be in the South, but it gets cold in the winters, probably because the Tidewater area is close to the ocean. In 1983 we

Dallas Cowboy cheerleaders

pulled out, headed to war. We were to replace another ship identical to ours called the Iwo Jima. We were headed to Beirut, Lebanon, where there was a war going on. We got there in two weeks. Before leaving we went to Parris Island in South Carolina and picked up 1,500 Marines. One of the highlights of this trip was when the Dallas Cowboys Cheerleaders came and did a show.

The Guadalcanal was the lead ship, so the event was on our ship. The cheerleaders were very nice. They were trying to get away from a certain lady who was in charge of them. They were sitting on guys' laps and taking photos. They were sneaking away. I met one black cheerleader who had come down below deck. She was with some Marines and I told her that this was my ship and I could show her around. She followed me down to our berthing area – where we slept. All the guys were surprised and happy to see her that far in the belly of the ship. I then took her to my machine shop. I showed her the engine room and the boiler room and took her to the very top of the ship. She was nice.

On October 23, 1983 there was a suicide bombing with two trucks that struck the barracks where our Marines were sleeping in Beirut, and 241 of our Marines died. I remember that evening. I was awoken to a muffled "Boom!" And then bells and whistles went off with, "General Quarters! General Quarters! All hands on deck — this is not a drill!" I got my clothes on and reported to the quarter deck. They said we had casualties coming aboard and we would need to help assist them to the ship's hospital. Marines started coming back aboard with half their clothes blown off, and the looks on their faces were pure shock. I carried about ten guys on stretcher and maybe five by just putting them in a bear hug and carrying them up to the hospital. The ship's hospital got full really quick and had to start taking the remaining Marines to hospitals on shore. I remember the shocked looks on their faces and the smell of burnt skin. When I finished the next day. I noticed how much blood and guts were on my clothes. My boots had been making a squishing noise because there was so much blood that had seeped down into them. I took the longest shower I had ever taken. All the guys were tired, and there were blood and guts all over the ship and a trail of blood and guts headed up to the hospital. I still have vivid memories of that night and morning.

We stayed in Lebanon for six months. Watching the tracers every day and night was tough. We were on the ship about one mile off the coast, and we could smell the sulfur of the guns. We were glad to set sail from there.

Mentors

When I thought about writing this book. I thought
of Anthony "Tony" Collins. I had read his book, "Broken
Road," and I decided to ask who his writer was. Her
name was Bethany Bradsher – check out her Instagram.
I contacted her and she seemed nice. I mentioned I was
three-fourths of the way finished and wanted her to
help me write. She agreed. I had also saw her Instagram
and saw she must have been cool with a lot of different
types of people. Anthony has a Tony Collins Foundation
Event, the Class of 1977 Celebrity Golf Classic in Penn
Yan. Check out Tonycollinsfoundation@gmail.com. Two
things stuck out for me in his book. I saw the numbers
on how many fans began going to ECU football games
for his Sophomore year versus his freshman season.
And not only was he the starting running back, he also
did kickoff returns. My other favorite stat on Anthony

was that he had a kickoff return of 100 yards against the mighty Florida State Seminoles. I remember Anthony growing up in the same area of upstate New York as me. I am from Geneva, a small town between Rochester and Syracuse in The Finger Lakes region. Anthony was from another small town in the Finger Lakes called Penn Yan, which is about twenty minutes from Geneva. Our high schools played each other. I graduated from GHS in 1975 and Anthony graduated from Penn Yan in 1977. I also remember his older brothers Sam and Morris. I believe and heard his brother Morris was the best of all the Collins boys. He is a well-respected guy.

Anthony also had a younger brother, Loyd, who was cooler than Anthony. (Just Kidding). But his younger brother sadly passed; he was a good kid and he passed away way too soon. He's missed. The only downside of Anthony's book was when Loyd did not want to go to football practice and Anthony beat him up. (LOL). Loyd was loud, and back then a lot of guys would bark like a dog. I'd have to say Loyd had the best bark of us all. Anthony came from a large family of athletes from Penn Yan. His brothers paved the way for him. In his book he said he dreamt/visioned playing in the NFL. He could hear the roar of the NFL crowd. He was destined. He was also a good basketball player and very good in track and field. I first saw him run the 20-yard dash at a track meet at Hobart College. He was making a sound like a choo-choo train. I also remember him playing summer league softball in Geneva. He was a speedster to the bases.

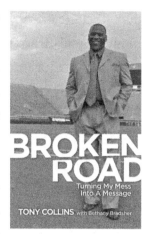

I also remember going to watch Anthony play during his college days at ECU. He dated my younger sister Brenda. The first time I saw him play in college I remember walking into the stadium with his name on the football board saying "Go A.C." I thought, *wow*, here's a small town kid who now has his name being flashed on the billboard before thousands of fans. I remember having a party at my house and I did not invite him although his family member Matt asked me. I was wrong for saying he was not invited; it still bothers me to this day. I mentioned this incident to him and apologized. He said, "Not to worry about that." Good guy. He now also lives here in N.C., and he has a golf tournament each year back in Penn Yan. When Anthony graduated from ECU he was not inducted into the ECU football hall until 2011. I felt Anthony had better numbers than most of the other running backs, and I wrote a letter to the ECU athletic department saying that I did not feel he was given his due. It's a great read. I read it three times. There are so many legends from my home town of Geneva, people who meant a lot to me. The first legend that comes to mind is a guy named Kipp Knittle. I first met Kipp at Prospect Avenue School around 1965 when I was nine, and I'll always remember him. He was a man amongst kids. Every one of us kids wanted to be around him. I used to push kids out of the way to be behind him in the lunch line. He treated all of us kids like his little brothers and sisters. He used to go straight to The Book Store/Barrody's on Exchange Street after school. (When he came to school, which was not often. A lot of the old bookies, Italian men hung out there, I believe they gambled and played cards. I used to follow him because I admired him and wanted to be like him. Plus, he lived on Middle Street and I lived at the end of Middle Street and Evans Street. I also wanted to talk like him. Kipp spoke with a lisp, so I used to try speaking with a lisp. I was only in contact with him for that one school year, but it was a major step in my life. I have a tattoo on my side of all the people I admire who have passed away, and I have Kipp Knittle's name tattooed, along with ten others.

I used to ask Kipp if I could walk home with him, but he said no. I was mad and wanted to beat him up but there was no way I could beat Kipp. Plus, I had to much respect to raise a hand to him. When he said no, I said, "OK Kipp, what about tomorrow? Can I walk home with you tomorrow?" He said, "Yea, Kiddo." He called all us kids Kiddo. I couldn't wait for tomorrow. I started bragging to the other kids saying, "Kipp said I can walk home with him tomorrow." "Ha-ha Kipp is MY friend not yours!!" I said this while sticking out my tongue. Tomorrow finally came. When I got to school I saw Kipp's desk empty, so I watched the clock. Eight 'o' clock Kipp's seat is empty, nine 'o' clock, ten 'o' clock. Once eleven 'o' clock came and his desk was still empty, I knew he was not coming. I was so hurt. When he finally came back to school, I was closest to him again. He always dressed well. He finally let me walk home with him a few times. Once he took me behind a building on the corner of North and Exchange Street. There is a parts store there and used to be an ice cream van there years ago. He took me back there, and I was so scared. I had never been behind a building like that. Back there Kipp showed me a pile of coins. Quarters, dimes, nickels and pennies. It looked knee-high. He told me to go ahead and get some. I reached down and took a nickel and a penny. He said I could get more, and I said, "No this is enough." We headed out and he said, "Don't ever, ever come back here again." I said OK. I used to see his sisters at the winter basketball games around 1976, when they came to watch Earl Palmeri play at the old Junior High. I also worked with one of his sisters at the Canandaigua Wine Company. Kipp Knittle was a giant. He died way too soon. In his short time on this earth he made big

Johnnie Ray

SECOND IMPACT
The Ray Ciancaglini Story
by Andy Siegel

What I'm currently reading

strides and touched a lot of lives. You can go anywhere in the Finger Lakes and mention his name, and people remember him. Kipp R.I.P..

I just ordered a book from another Geneva guy: Second Impact (The Ray Ciancaglini Story) by Andy Siegel. Ray was a good boxer who was a few years ahead of me in high school.

Mr. Johnnie Ray White Sr. is the next Geneva Legend. Johnnie Ray came to Geneva from Florida. They first moved in a big white house near Chartres Homes before they moved to 77 Middle Street – aka The Mecca of Geneva. I remember the very first day I came home from prison. I made sure that I went to 77 Middle Street. On my first day home after being gone for twenty years that was an important

place to visit and impor-
tant folks to be around
– Princess and Johnnie
Ray White. In prison we
learn people, places and
things. Things couldn't
have been better than
being with my big broth-
er Barron at 77 Middle
Street with Princess and
Johnnie Ray White. I
made sure that I got up
and spoke at this funeral.
He was a true great. His
name and legacy will
never die in Geneva. I
hung around his son Tat
for many years; he was
my best friend.

Ralph Fratto

Ralph Fratto and Roberto Duran

Mr. Ralph Fratto Sr. is another living legend of
Geneva. I first met Mr. Ralph Fratto, Sr. around 1970 at
the Civic Center on the corner of Main and Castle streets.
He and a guy named Ralph Fryer were teaching boxing.
I was told about Mr. Fratto before meeting him. I was
told he was a well-respected Italian man. I got there and
got beat really bad by a seasoned boxing veteran named

Walter Russ. I quickly learned that boxing was not for me. Throughout the years I knew who Mr. Fratto was and made sure that if I saw him, I spoke. He had a son named Ralph Jr. Ralph was a good boxer and us blacks liked him. Ralph had a cousin that had a smart lip and a lot of us blacks wanted to beat his ass, but we didn't due to the respect we had for the Fratto family. My locker in school was always near Lesley Fratto because our last names began with the same letters. She was very nice; she and my sister Barbara became friends and still are to this day. I saw and spoke with Lesley at the 40-year class reunion.

There is an old saying – you do not know who your friends are until your back is against the wall. Well, when I was incarcerated at Groveland Correctional Facility in around 2001 I was called to go to a visit. I went to the visiting room expecting to see family. I walked in the visiting room and saw none of my family. I soon heard an Italian voice saying, "Hey Bronson." It was Mr. Fratto! He said "Bronson, come over and sit." I felt shame, guilt and embarrassment. For a guy like him to come and visit me, I was honored but I felt shame. He was there to also see another person and decided to see us both. (Me first). He stayed for about an hour. Mr. Fratto spoke about God and the church. I was surprised that he mentioned our higher powers. At that time, I was not doing very well. He asked me if I needed anything and

I said no, because I was too ashamed to ask. He spoke to me for a bit and was gone. He placed $20 into my account for commissary. I felt honored for a long time after that visit. It meant a lot to me.

Mr. Wilmer Alexander II and the Dukes were definitely living legends. I once heard a radio announcer from WBBF, the oldies jazz station in Rochester, saying that Wilmer Alexander and the Dukes should be in the Rock and Roll Hall of Fame. I thought that was a huge compliment. I remember when my dad passed away

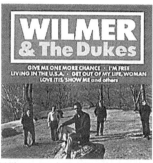

Wilmer and The Dukes album cover

Sam Passalaqua handing a stool, which was a type of trophy, to my brother Brian.

in 1969, my brother Butch had to come home from the Army for the funeral. I remember him telling my sister Beth that he heard Wilmer Alexander II and the Dukes on the radio where he was stationed in Korea. That was the first time I heard that name mentioned. I also heard his name mentioned because my oldest sister Bonita was a hellraiser. When I was young, I remember someone telling me that my sister Bonita was always starting fights at the Club 86 when Wilmer Alexander II and the Dukes played. I felt bad that my sister was the person who was spoiling a good time for others. To this day, I always remind her of that person telling me that about her. She was trouble then and she is trouble today. Around 1972 I was at the house that is on the corner of Wadsworth and Middle, which is where they lived. I remember seeing a very beautiful lady get out of her car and walk into the house. She was outstanding. I thought, "Wow, only stars get ladies that beautiful." I guessed she must have been friends with Wilmer Alexander II.

A few other Geneva legends:

Mr. Sam Passalaqua Sr.: As a youngster I used to hang around one of his children Gary. There was also Steve and Mona, however many other Passalaqua. They lived over by Club 86. I think Avenue D area. He was a great pee wee league coach. He coached the Packers. They were the pee wee team to beat.

Mr. Sully Morabito: I first met this legend when I worked with him at the American Can Company. I first took notice of him when he voiced his opinion at a Union meeting. I thought wow, I better pay attention to this guy. And he had a walk that said, 'Do not F with me'. He and his wife had a restaurant next door to the American Can. I went there at times for a burger. His wife was a nice lady. I remember two boys and one girl in that family. They lived down the road on Gambie Road. Sue Seymore lived near them.

Al Lisi

John Williams and his wife Carrie.

One of his son's was a Correctional Officer at Auburn Correctional Facility and escorted me to my mom's funeral from Auburn C.F. in 1991. The Marchenese boys and Rodney Sabatini lived out that way also.

Mr. Al Lisi: Al Lisi ran one of the most troubled - happening bars in Geneva History. Al's bar was open for years. It had it's ups and down but it survived. And who owned it? One of the toughest-respected men in Geneva history – Al Lisi. He also had three daughters Edeen, Barb and Jeannie. Edeen was very beautiful/popular and a cheerleader. The middle sister was Barb. I had no idea until I worked with Barb at the Canandaigua

Lonnie and Lucille Mallard

Veterans Administration that she used to call the black girls a Nigger in high school. I laughed. She admitted to saying it and admitted to getting her ass beat. She and I were cool.

The youngest was Jeannie. She was very beautiful and a cheerleader. Jeannie dated guy that spoke on the C.B. Radio, lived close to the corner of North and Genesee.

Mr. John Henry Williams: Mr. John Henry Williams is a legend in Geneva also. He had numerous children and was a tall and outspoken man - He spoke him mind. His sons were Butch, Ricky and Jerome. His daughters were Peggy, Jonnie Mae, and Lilly Bell.

Mr. Lonnie Mallard: Lonnie is a living legend that most people in Geneva know. I first met him during my sophomore high school years. I remember him coming to the basketball games. He attended most sporting events in Geneva. He is married to Ms. Lucille Mallard who is the NAACP President. His children are Larry,

Vincent and Val Mallard. He is a well-respected man. I remember him being at all the GHS basketball games and sports events. They had a dog named Dino that was a terrorizer. Dino was a huge German Sheppard. He would break the chain at home on Prospect Avenue, head downtown, go and get another huge German Sheppard on Tillman Street. It was Junior Yancey's dog. Those two dogs would walk down Exchange Street like they owned it. When Dino headed home I remember seeing him on the Corner of North and Exchange Street, sitting down watching the traffic light until it turned green then he headed across the street to home, just like a human. Vincent Mallard used to work at Kentucky Fried Chicken there on that corner. I first remember Lonnie and Lucille Mallard when the lived behind Daniels Den. They also had a dog back there. Us kids used to use that little alley to walk down. When I first came home from incarceration he was one of the first who welcomed me back home. Lonnie is a living legend. I am honored to know him. I asked Lonnie what would he like the people to know about him. He said he wanted me to write that he enjoyed helping people – from adults to children.

Mr. John Serafine Sr.: I first remember this giant when I graduated from high school 1975. My mom came to me saying some man by the name of Mr. Serafine approached her in reference to be possibly

Mother Freedom Band

becoming a State Trooper. Through the years I always whenever I saw him we always had a very nice short conversation. The last time I saw him was at CCFL his son John had a high school game against Geneva High in 1976. Again we stopped and chatted for a bit. He was a nice and respected man. I later saw he was not feeling well and how much love and respect he had being a State Trooper. R.I.P. Mr. Serafine.

Mr. Jimmy Richmond Jr.: Jimmy Richmond Jr. is a guy most people in Geneva knows because he was a leader of a local band named the Echomen. I remember going to their dances back around 1970. The best where when they played at the Civic Center. Jimmy still plays to this day and plays organ at The Mount Olive Missionary Baptist Church in Geneva. He has a brother Randy and two sister's Rhonda and Michelle. His mom past a few years ago who was a very nice lady. I enjoyed hearing her sing for the choir at Church. R.I.P. Ms. Peg Richmond. Jimmy's dad also still sings for the choir; he's a nice man.

Life's tragedies can sometimes be helpful. It really teaches you a lot about people in general. I never thought most of the people who are my friends now would be there for me when my friends I hung around most of my life would not.

Me and Amy Chaplin

40th class reunion: I graduated from GHS in 1975, and I did make the 1980 reunion. I attempted to make the 35th class reunion while on parole. I met with my parole officer and was told that I was not allowed to go to the class reunion. There was really no reason – just no. But I did make it to the 40th class reunion that was held at the American Legion. I arrived and the first person I saw walking in was Ms. Amy Chaplin. Amy (in my book) is the most respected person in our class. I had intentions on speaking – apologizing to Amy for the crimes that I committed. You see – when we do things that are bad or good, there are certain people who stand out. I did something bad, and Amy Chaplin was a person that made me feel worse – more shame and more embarrassment. She was also entering with her husband, who I played summer lacrosse with. He's a nice guy and a lucky guy to have Amy as a wife. During my incarceration I imagined the day when I saw Amy and how was I going to approach her and how I was going to apologize for my crimes. I practiced that event many times in my cells. I finally got the chance to apologize to her at the class reunion but I got too nervous. I did speak with her and took a photo with her later that evening, but I never got the chance to apologize.

After the reunion I contacted Nancy Colluzzi and asked her if she could get me Amy's email. I wanted to email Amy to apologize. It never happened and to this day, I kick myself for not apologizing to her. I waited twenty years to see Amy and blew it. Amy is the most popular person in our class and one of the most respected in Geneva. Everyone loved Amy, Alanis Morissette reminds me of Amy. Amy and I go way back, not only to high school, but after high school she attended a college called Herkimer that was thirty minutes from the college I attended, Fulton Montgomery Community College. She came to visit me once with Judy Knapp and Nancy Colluzzi, and one weekend I drove to Herkimer and brought her back to my college. Every city and town has people who are well-respected. In my book, Amy

Chaplin is the White Queen of Geneva. The Black Queen of Geneva is a girl named Trishia White. The Spanish Queen of Geneva is a beautiful lady named Doris Diaz.

Trishia White

I remember her from a young age. She was beautiful. She had a relative, Vivian Fuentes, who came to Geneva from Puerto Rico, and I dated her for a short time.

I also saw Peter Hashem at the class reunion – he had a nice-looking wife. I remember he had a small hut in the back of his house — I partied back there once. Peter has a brother named Michael who is now a famous jazz player. Joey Sharp was there also. I saw that he married one of the prettiest girls in Geneva history. She had a sister and they grew up on Brooks Street. I graduated with another jazz musician named Dan Ferris, who later changed his name to Carl Ferris. I hear he plays on the Las Vegas strip.

My conclusion is simple: It's in one of my poems. Listen...

I came from a very good family. When my dad passed I had no guidance, so I strayed into hanging around troubled youths. Whatever negativity you start to internalize in a small way, it grows and grows. You

In prison shirt

become more daring, rather it's drugs or burglaries. My stealing eight-track tapes from cars in 1972 led me to stealing bikes, to burglaries during Spring Breaks, to breaking into empty houses, to wanting more of a challenge and breaking in while someone was at home, to committing a sex offense. Originally I wanted my book to be named, "All-American Kid Gone Bad."

Completing twenty-two years of incarceration was not easy. However, there's a rapper/hip-hop artist named Biggie Smalls and in one of his songs, which is about his release from pris-on, the prison guard says, "Yea, you'll be back, just like the others," and Biggie replies, "Not me, I've got plans — big plans." I used to say that to myself all the time. I can honestly say that I'm a success story. How many ex-cons who completed twenty-two years of incarceration as a sex offender can say that they are now a homeowner, as well as a landlord, the president of a veterans committee for all city employees, and working a great job for the city where they live?

It takes drive and determination to make a comeback. It also takes a lot of networking. I would like to add that the biggest mistake I made was not asking for help. Once we find ourselves being faced with a problem, we are often afraid to ask for help. Asking for help is a difficult thing to do. Ask for help if you find yourself facing a problem in life. It can save your life and the lives of others.

BRONSON

Acknowledgements

Shout-outs: I want to give a shout-out to Rodney Sabatini, Tim Kelly, John George's mom Phyllis Snyder, Lisa Georgiani, Duke Coleman, Tat White, Ms. Carol Cosentino, Anthony Liberatore (Ralph and Carol's son), Cindy Campbell-Ludwig, John and Jay VanHouten - (John beat me up once in 1973 high school and chipped my tooth), Lori Rickerson, Lainney Marino, and Stephanie Quataro. Also Katrina Graham, Mike Palmeri, John Quathera, Gayle Ricker, Carol and James Rinaldo, Ms. Dale Easton, Susan Fegley, LuAnn Gillotti, Jeannie Lisi, Sharon Daniels and Edna Johnson.

Also a shout-out to the Holy Trinity, my two angels since birth - Trinity and Sebastian.

My favorite bible verse is Joshua 1:1-18. I was baptized while at Gowanda C.F. by being submerged into water.

Duplex I purchased

I often hear people say how hard it is to succeed. I tell them look, if I can do 22 years of incarceration and be released as a sex offender, become the President of a Veterans Committee for all city employees, become a landlord and home owner. Anyone can do anything. All you need is drive, to remain hungry and network. You can do anything..

I'd like to encourage all of my readers to write a book. Tell your story. Everyone has a story to tell. I encourage you to tell yours. Your book does not necessarily have to begin at childhood. It should begin where your thoughts begin when you think of your past. Once you begin there, the rest will fall into place. And once you start telling your story, you cannot stop. It's also therapeutic.

As my friend Devra Rivkin would say:

Peace…

Devra Rivkin

Today Bronson is living in Garner, North Carolina, where he has been since 2014. He has worked for Interstate Battery, the Veterans Administration, Autozone and the City of Durham N.C. He is the president of the Veterans Committee for The Durham City Employees. Favorite Movies: Platoon, Straight Outta Compton and My Girl 1. Favorite pasttimes: Napping and the Gym, Favorite Songs: 5 'o' clock by Nonchalant, To Sir with Love by: Lu Lu, Every time you go away by Paul Young, Best Part by Leah Jenea, Video on youtube of Christopher Duffley singing Open the eyes of my Heart and A song for you by Justin Timberlake. Favorite Food: Spaghetti and meatballs. Favorite Books: Marine Sniper by Charles Henderson, Esoteric Encyclopedia of Eternal Knowledge by Vernon Howard, also books on the Underground Railroad and the slave trade. Favorite Authors: James Patterson and Sylvia Brown.

Find Bronson on:

Email: bronsonf7@gmail.com

Instagram: str8.315.919

LinkedIn: https://www.linkedin.com/in/bronsonfrank/

Website: ceremonialwhitebirds.com

Made in the USA
Las Vegas, NV
26 July 2021

27080066R00098